Claire Gillman has been a professional writer for more than 25 years. In that time, she has written 23 non-fiction and creative fiction books for adults and children. She was the editor of several women's consumer magazines before changing tack to become a regular freelance contributor to many leading magazines and national newspapers, most notably the *Guardian* and *The Times.*

Claire is an editor for The Writers' Workshop, regularly writing critiques and discussing manuscripts to help writers towards publication. She also leads writers' workshops and writing groups in various locations, always with the emphasis on fun, style, relaxation and discovering your inner creativity.

Latest books by Claire Gillman

Revenge is Sweet: Stories of Retribution and Revenge
Make Money From Freelance Writing
Write Fantastic Non-Fiction and Get it Published
You and Your Ageing Parents: How to Balance Your Needs
and Theirs

The Best of Boys

■ ■ ■

*Helping your sons through
their teenage years*

Claire Gillman

Published in 2013 by Albert Bridge Books

Copyright © 2013, Claire Gillman

ISBN: 978-1-909771-01-7

To my husband, Nick
and our sons, Alex and George

Acknowledgements

I would like to thank everyone who has contributed to the creation of this book – from the professional experts who gave up their valuable time, through the team of volunteer parents who endured endless questioning, to the enthusiastic young men who agreed to speak so candidly about their personal experiences of growing up. In particular, I'd like to thank those who told their personal stories for this book and to mention Dr Dinah Jayson and Charmian Evans who gave unflaggingly of their time, advice and support. Also, to Adrienne Katz, for her cooperation and for her invaluable report from The Tomorrow's Men project.

Contents

Introduction

There has never been a more confusing or difficult time in which to be male. Traditional roles have changed, 'girl power' is in the ascendancy (with girls outperforming boys at school), and male unemployment and street violence is on the increase.

Parents want the best for their children, whatever the gender, and the increased efforts to advance women and girls are to be applauded. Yet there is no doubt that boys have an uncertain future too, and that they need careful and attentive raising. Parents of boys naturally want them to grow up happy, self-confident, and well-balanced and yet they face a minefield of political correctness and gender preconceptions, and sons are often far less communicative than daughters.

As a parent, you may find yourself confused by your son's behaviour on more occasions than you would care to confess, and frankly at a loss about how to cope. Do you sometimes feel that life is a constant battle and that you are losing? If parenting for you is synonymous with any of the following emotions, then help is at hand.

Do you sometimes feel:

- Helpless?
- Ignored?
- Drained?

- Lacking in control?
- Inadequate?
- Unappreciated?
- Misunderstood?
- Confused?

There are times when your son can make you feel one or many of the above emotions, but it is important to hold on to the positive moments. It is time to stop comparing your kids to their 'perfect' cousins/classmates/next-door neighbour (delete as appropriate), and to start exploring ways to enjoy them and make the most of your family time together.

This book is aimed at parents of boys aged nine to eighteen years old. It is written as one mother talking to another because that is largely how it was researched. However, the information included is just as relevant to any fathers reading the book. The topics, which range from the physical and emotional changes of puberty through to gap year travel, are intended to help you to understand your son's particular needs and to recognize that there are many ways in which you can help him to grow into a happy and healthy adult. It explains how best to relate to your son, how to get through the rough times, particularly the adolescent years, and it suggests ways in which to tackle many of the boy-related issues and difficulties.

How this book can help you

Raising sons can be wonderfully rewarding, but it can be challenging. As a parent, you can benefit from sharing ideas and take comfort in knowing that others are undergoing similar experiences, whether that be the muscle-flexing and testing of the pre-teens (nine to eleven years), the angst of early adolescence (twelve to fourteen years) or the dangers of new-found freedoms (fifteen to eighteen years).

In the light of alarming statistics regarding depression and suicide in young men, parents want as much information and advice as possible on helping their sons to develop into happy, healthy young men. An array of parenting techniques and tools can help you to make informed decisions about which style of parenting will work best for you and your children.

This book provides practical ideas from experts and other parents, solace, and support. It will help you to escape the knee-jerk reaction to a situation and give you ideas for a thought-out response.

Whether you decide to opt for small changes or a radically different approach to family life, this book will help you to look at things in a new way. It will help you to make life for you and your sons more fun and fulfilling. The aim of the book is to:

- **Help you to keep things in perspective.** When you see your son with his peers, you soon appreciate that he is no worse than any other boy. More to the point, you are not alone in how you feel – many parents are experiencing exactly the same feelings and reactions to their sons.
- **Help you to appreciate his ways.** Like all children, boys are individuals, and your support and acceptance will allow him to develop his own unique characteristics and the self-confidence to be his own person. Your son does not have to conform to a 'prescription personality' to be an acceptable male.

- **Help you to help your son**. We would all like the best possible relationship with our sons and to be able to give them the guidance, support, and advice that enables them to realize their potential. This book can help you to achieve that ambition.
- **Help you to stop beating yourself up**. You are not necessarily a bad parent just because your son is unruly/ uncommunicative/ disobedient/ lacking in motivation/ too soft etc., etc., and blaming yourself is not helping you or your son.
- **Help you to remember that no one gets it right all the time**. We live in the real world and we all make mistakes. The most important thing is that you are trying. Move on from your mistakes and learn from them.
- **Help to give you confidence**. When you are having a dreadful time, it will help you to understand why you feel the way you do, examine why we react as we do, and offer ways in which to deal with your feelings.

Why this author?

As a mother of sons and a health writer, I do not have all the answers. But I do have the same questions. Daily, I face the same trials and challenges as other parents of young boys. However, as a journalist, I have access to many of the leading experts in the fields of child psychology, development and education, and the latest research findings. Moreover, my husband is a director of a charity that works with young people at risk and he has a wealth of practical experience and research material on hand.

And, just as valuable in many ways, I have an excuse to speak to many other parents of sons about their expectations and experiences, and I find out what works for them. We can all benefit from the know-how of other parents who have been through it already and, most importantly, it really helps to realize that you are not alone.

The information included in this book was gleaned from many different sources – from psychiatrists, child and adolescent educational experts, and from parents who hail from all sorts of different family units and backgrounds. Furthermore, for a real eye-opener, there are comments scattered throughout the book collected from the numerous young men that I interviewed and these give some glorious insights.

The majority of parents of boys experience the same range of feelings and emotions, to varying degrees, and all find different ways to cope with the downsides and to make the very most of the good moments.

This is not a didactic manual for raising sons that offers a prescriptive package of skills guaranteed to make you 'a good parent'. Like most right-thinking people, I am very sceptical of the 'universal panacea' approach to parenting, and I acknowledge that what works for one family may be anathema to another. Being a 'good parent' is not quantifiable and every family relationship is unique.

However, this book can offer you a variety of strategies to enrich your lives together. You can digest the suggestions and pick and choose the strategies that best resonate with you, your parenting style, your temperament, and your son's personality.

It is so easy to lose sight of the pleasure of parenting, but raising boys does not have to be a battle – it can be great fun. This book is a celebration of the good things about being male as well as offering advice to deal with some of the more worrying aspects of boys' behaviour!

I hope and expect that you will find some strategies in this book that will make the family experience more pleasurable and more effective for both you and your son. In this book, we prefer to concentrate on enjoying the positive side of boys' masculinity, rather than quashing it. Remember, there is no right or wrong way to raise your sons, just better ways to make the experience more fulfilling for everyone.

1

Slugs, snails and puppy dogs' tails: what it is to be male

It must be hard for young men today who recognize that many traditional male qualities that were valued in the past have turned from assets to liabilities. The aggression, vitality and courage needed to fight wars and defend the homestead are of little use in a sedentary, sanitized modern lifestyle. Yet any parent of boys will tell you that those characteristics are still apparent in their developing sons. So where do young men find an outlet for such qualities? Well, for some, who combine these vigorous attributes with the frustration of an unpromising and unchallenging future, the surging increase in street crime and violence is an unsurprising outcome.

Add to this the fact that girls are outstripping boys in education and competing equally in the job market, and you can see why boys are confused about what it is to be male and about what their future holds. In fact, 58 per cent of young men think that it is harder for men these days.

What else do young men think about their role and their future in our modern times?

> I accept girls doing better than guys. If you know you
> are working hard, it's hard to fight it.
>
> *Seventeen-year-old*

Strong, silent types

Leading Lads, by Adrienne Katz, Ann Buchanan and Anne
McCoy (Young Voice, 2002), is the report of the Tomorrow's Men project, and it tells what is really going on in
the heads of 1,400 young men across Britain. The aim
of the project was to talk to boys who are confident and
optimistic about life (the Can-do Boys) and compare them
with those who are not (the Low Can-do Boys). The results
on their views about masculinity are very revealing and
concur with the feedback from the young men interviewed
for this book.

It seems that not only are boys worried that the future is
looking less assured for them but, to make matters worse,
they find it difficult to voice their concerns. As the parent of
boys, it is a real worry to learn that, among those interviewed,
there is a widespread belief that 'if you're dying inside, no
one must know'. Very few boys, about one-third in total, talk
to someone or are able to express how they feel when things
are getting on top of them. They prefer instead to bottle up
their emotions and to try to disguise the fact that they are
feeling low.

And just to compound things, many felt that they were
offered very little in the way of help. By contrast, parents
tend to pick up on and respond to girls' distress more readily, firstly because it is more evident, but also because girls

tend to rely on a stronger network of emotional support from family and friends.

> Women have got more self-esteem. I think young men feel threatened. *Eighteen-year-old*

Boys, however, see such a network as a weakness and the role of friendship for them is vastly different than it is for girls. 'I wouldn't talk to a friend about a problem – most boys wouldn't. He's a mate – for having a laugh and that,' summarizes one interviewee.

Thankfully, this go-it-alone approach seems to mellow slightly as boys reach their late teens. By this stage they have a couple of close friends within their circle to whom they feel they can trust their inner thoughts and feelings. Nevertheless, this trust has to be earned over a period of time and, even so, boys are still reluctant to talk about their most private fears because they do not wish to be seen as weak by those they respect and love.

If younger boys are going to spill the beans about how they are feeling to anyone, it will most likely be to their mothers, but the likelihood of this happening depends largely on how confident the boy feels about himself. Seventy-six per cent of Can-do Boys say that they would turn to their mother as their primary source of emotional support, in contrast to only 44 per cent of Low Can-do Boys.

Unfortunately, you cannot breathe a sigh of relief just yet because having a close relationship with your son is not a cast-iron guarantee that he will confide his troubles in you.

Paradoxically, many boys think that it is manly to protect their parents and to shoulder problems by themselves. Thus, if your son is a caring boy and you enjoy a close relationship, he may keep a lid on his distress because he feels the need to protect you.

Parental and cultural influence
So, how do boys come by these notions that it is manly to keep your troubles to yourself and that men should sort out their own problems? Surely this is outmoded thinking?

Without even realizing it, as parents, we constantly send our children messages about what it is to be male and female. From the clothes you wear to the way you interact with your partner and friends, everything about you and your partner influences your son's understanding of masculinity and femininity.

For example, research shows that if fathers do not speak about their emotions or relationships, then sons believe that this is how men should behave. Despite all the recent exhortations for men to get in touch with their inner feelings, if your partner or the important men in your son's life do not guide him by example, showing him how they handle their emotions, then he will deduce from their behaviour that stoicism is manly. (See Chapter Seven for more details on dealing with emotions.)

It may be hard for you to identify and evaluate the power of the parental messages that you give your son, yet if you are aware of your interpretation of masculinity, you can better understand your expectations of him and use that knowledge constructively. However, are you aware of your true interpretation of masculinity and femininity?

Seeking help

Given that a boy will not confide in his friends and tries his hardest to protect his parents, who can he turn to in times of need? The *Leading Lads* survey asked if boys would phone a helpline if they were extremely upset and, somewhat worryingly, almost three-quarters of Can-do Boys said that they would not. Of this group, more than half said, 'It's my business and I must sort it out.'

If your son tends to put a brave face on things and is unlikely to turn to you, you can urge him to seek help from a professional helpline if things get really bad by stressing the manly characteristics that making such a call involves, namely:

- It takes courage to pick up the phone.
- It is a positive, action-oriented step that should appeal to his masculine side.
- He would be taking control of the situation.
- A helpline is confidential and his privacy is protected.
- It is a masculine thing to do.
- If he wants to spare you and his loved ones, this is a possible solution.

Your gender expectations are deeply ingrained and were formed in your own infancy from the cues provided by your parents and from society at large. These views of what is masculine and what is feminine become internalized and, in turn, are passed on to your son.

Genetic gender differences
In light of the traditional role of man as protector, it is ironic to think that males are more vulnerable than females, both in the womb and in life. Although 120 males are conceived for every 100 females, because male embryos are more fragile there is a greater chance of miscarriage. By the time the babies are born, the differential has dropped to 106 boy babies for every 100 girls.

As a parent of a son, what is more worrying is that once born, the vulnerability remains. Every year, twice as many boys die as girls, mostly because more are killed on the road. However, non-violent causes of death (such as muscular dystrophy and cancers such as leukaemia) are also more prevalent in boys than in girls. Basically, boys and men are more susceptible than girls and women to many disorders, including cerebral palsy, autism, and certain learning difficulties such as dyslexia, and inherited conditions such as colour blindness. It is believed that the reason for this is that the male XY chromosome combination is less robust and has a weaker immune system than the female XX combination.

Are there any genetic pluses for boys? Well, the obvious genetic difference is that the average boy has 30 per cent more muscle bulk than the average girl. Boys are stronger and they were built for action – they even have more red blood cells than their female counterparts.

Most amazing of all gender differences is that it is now known that boys' and girls' brain development differs and this has huge ramifications for boys in education (see Chapter Nine).

333333

In a television series presented by Dr Robert Winston, *Child of Our Time*, 2000, parents were given an unfamiliar baby to hold and to entertain with a variety of provided props. Unbeknown to the unsuspecting guinea pigs, the babies' identities had been swapped: boy babies were in girls' clothing and vice versa. The reactions of the parents were filmed and, almost universally, parents reached for gender-specific toys to comfort their unfamiliar charges.

In another study, adults were presented with a baby whose gender was ambiguous. When the parents were told the baby was a boy, they tended to speak and play in a rough, horse-play manner and, with a girl, they were more gentle – even cooing in a higher voice. If we start to differentiate between the genders from such a tender age, no wonder our understanding of what it is to be male and female becomes so entrenched, even as a child.

To break out of the gender expectation mould is hard, despite your best intentions, but it is even harder for your son who so desperately wants to fit in and be accepted. Even if you give your son permission to choose the kind of boy he wants to be, to flout stereotypical convention is extremely difficult, especially when there is considerable external pressure on him, both cultural and from peers, to conform.

What you can do
- Encourage your son to talk about how he feels from a young age and discourage the bottling up of distress.
- Recognize your gender expectations and make sure your instincts do not contradict what you are saying to your son – he will spot the double standards.
- Help him to learn how to manage emotions and anger in particular (see Chapter Seven).

- Do not try to suppress your son's physicality. He needs exercise, so try to build time for a walk, a kick about in the park or some sport into his daily routine.
- Do not discourage or be worried about your son showing 'feminine' qualities – remember to loosen the 'genderscript' that dictates his behaviour as often as possible.
- Be aware of your son's male role models. He has to get his ideas of what constitutes being male from somewhere and it is better this is from positive masculine input rather than leaving it to the media or to chance.
- Provide him with information that gives him some sense of control over a problem.
- Recognize your attitudes and prejudices about 'macho' or 'feminine' behaviour in boys and try to appreciate your son for who he is rather than what you expect him to be.
- Remember that boys and girls grow up with common experiences and common anxieties, and that there are many more similarities than differences between the sexes. Instil respect for girls and explain that neither gender is superior – just different.

> There is a danger in heading towards equality rather than meritocracy. Some skills women have are better than men and vice versa. You shouldn't have equality for the sake of it. *Eighteen-year-old*

■ PROBLEM SOLVING

My son cannot live up to my expectations

Everyone has a unique imprint in their mind of what it means to be male or female, which they have gleaned from their upbringing and the cultural influences they have experienced. Moreover, when your child is born, whatever the gender, you have certain expectations of how he or she will behave. Even if the messages that society sends out contradict your preconditioned ideas, you will find it very hard not to judge your son by those inbuilt and uniquely personal standards. The problem arises when your son does not conform to your ideals of masculinity and your expectations of him.

Each generation wants their children to improve on their achievements. So, if you were a sporting champ, a whiz at numbers or a musical maestro, you would probably have high hopes that your son will be even more accomplished in those areas. Unfortunately, it does not always work that way because of a little known biological principle called 'regression to the mean'.

Although, generally speaking, tall parents have tall children and short parents have short children, the tendency is for the next generation to be closer to the average than their parents, i.e. very tall parents will have children who are shorter than they are. This applies to other inherited characteristics such as athleticism, intelligence, and musicality.

Basically, just because you are outstandingly bright, you cannot necessarily expect your son to be a genius. You may be very athletic and equate masculinity with sporting aggression and ability, while your son hates competitive sport, cannot run for toffee, and prefers to excel at chess.

If you can accept the biological inevitability of 'regression to the mean', it may help you to let go of unfair hopes for your son and the inherent disappointment that unreasonable expectations entail. Naturally, you will still want the best for him, but outstanding ability is inborn, and you should not lose sight of that undeniable truth.

What you can do
- Try to keep your expectations realistic.
- Do not live vicariously through your child.
- Value your son for what he is, not because he might fulfil your ambitions.
- Challenge your inbuilt understanding of masculinity whenever it causes you to be critical of your son.

Looking ahead
Where does this rather bleak picture of modern masculinity leave a teenage boy who is about to pass into manhood? Have men completely lost the plot? And what, if anything, can parents of sons do about it?

Well, the facts are indisputable. Boys are failing in schools. There is an increase in street violence and attacks on and by young men. Teenage boys do get into trouble with the law and take risks. And, sadly, suicide is the second most common cause of death among young men aged fifteen to twenty-four. This supports the findings that boys find it difficult to talk about their problems or to seek emotional support.

However, raising a son in this climate does not have to be a grim prospect and none of these outcomes are inevitabilities. It is undeniable that boys face a more uncertain future than in days gone by, but there are also more freedoms and

> Girls get better qualifications. I don't think we're privileged because we're men. *Sixteen-year-old*

opportunities for those brave enough to grasp them. There is still plenty of scope for good male qualities to be used to great effect to benefit both the individual and society at large. With the right guidance, your son will grow into the sort of man whose masculine attributes do him credit and bring him fulfilment and joy.

If you can equip your son with the skills to face his problems and deal with them, to talk about his emotions and to turn adversity into opportunity, then you are doing him a huge service. Boys come equipped with a natural exuberance, boundless energy, optimism, and vitality for life. With the skills discussed in later chapters, you can help your son to harness his energies and his competitive spirit, and to channel them into something positive. You can help him to identify his powerful emotions and to deal with them constructively. He can build on the strengths of his natural male characteristics and use them to be the best he can be – and you can help him to find ways to do this. The future for men in general may be less well defined but, with your support, your son can be his own person, and can make sure that his prospects are bright and promising.

■ **CASE STUDY – Johnny's story**
It's only with hindsight that men reflect on entering manhood.

'I don't think there's any specific time when you cross a threshold and become a man. I think it's more about how you feel about yourself. It's a bit like wearing a big pair of

> Good male qualities are leadership, confidence and an ability to motivate others. *Eighteen-year-old*

leather shoes: when you're too small to fit the big shoes, they feel ungainly. As you get older and learn more, so the shoes become more comfortable. Becoming a man is more a case of feeling your way as you go along.

'You're moving from that gangly, full of energy phase to the cool phase where you don't really know who or what you are yourself, but you're trying desperately to pick up on all the signals that society gives out about what you have to do to be a man.

'If you look at me, I personally jumped through all the right hoops and got all the badges that meant I was a man. I was 6 feet 1 inch (1.9 m) and 15 stone (95 kg), a high-school jock, captain of the rugby team and head boy. It should have been easy to say that I had passed the "manhood" threshold, but it doesn't exist as a definitive line.

'Looking back, I may have had all of the accoutrements of manhood but I don't think I felt like a man until I knew I could be responsible for all of me – both physically and emotionally. That meant taking responsibility for my actions and how they impacted on others. Realistically, that was probably some time in my twenties.

'In traditional societies, you have a rite of passage or initiation ceremony where the senior men help you pass from boyhood to manhood, probably with some kind of physical challenge, and then everyone treats you like a man. I suppose our equivalent is taking that physical energy that you used to climb trees and stuff, and channelling it into pushing boundaries and taking risks – it's about riding motor-bikes, parachuting and being reckless. And testing yourself against other men, which I suppose never stops. As a teen-ager, it's about who can drink the most beer in the fastest time, and who can sing the bawdiest songs and offend the most people – and you do it because of this competitive edge that men have throughout their lives. It can become quite counterproductive as you get older – there's always that lurking aggression between men.

'Confronting other young men's anger comes as a shock to you. Part of being a man is learning to deal with that, but realizing that you can also get very angry yourself.

'Manhood is definitely how you feel about yourself, but it's also to do with taking responsibility for your actions and for who you are, as well. If you lose your temper, then you have to take the consequences on the chin. Once you start taking responsibility for your actions and for yourself, then you deal with things more rationally and hopefully prevent the more unsavoury aspects of male behaviour.

'It's a male characteristic to judge yourself against your heroes. But your heroes change and they are pretty indicative of the phase of life you are in. As a young lad, your heroes are your dad and sporting stars, but when you're becoming a man, you look to people who have achieved good things, or maybe, when you're older, people who've just achieved a good balance in their lives.

'I suppose most people think that becoming a man is something to do with having sex, but it's probably more to do with knowing the difference between enjoying having sex with someone and loving somebody. It's a distinction that some men fail to make throughout their life.

'When I say being a man is about knowing what your responsibilities are, it's also knowing that there's a responsibility to maintain yourself and to be able to have fun. I think most blokes need to have some excitement in their life, whether it be edge, competition, whatever it is that continues to let them feel that they are a bloke in their own right.'

2

Puberty and the way he looks

Apart from the infant stage, the greatest physical and emotional changes that you will ever witness in your sons take place during the developmental stage known as puberty.

The official definition of puberty is the age at which the secondary sexual characteristics start to appear and, in boys, the first outward sign of its onset is usually a sudden and acute growth spurt. They may already have a light dusting of straight wispy pubic hair while they are still relatively small but, since adolescents become intensely private, you may not know about that.

For most boys, puberty starts at around twelve, although it is considered normal if it begins any time from the age of nine to fourteen. In fact, you only have to look at a class of twelve-year-old boys to see that there is enormous diversity in the onset of their physical development. You could find a fresh-faced, diminutive lad with a high voice sitting alongside a gangly boy sporting a nascent moustache and gravelly voice, and yet they are probably the best of friends.

It is worth bearing in mind that although one boy may be physically more advanced than his classmates, he is not necessarily capable of acting 'more grown up' since physical and emotional development do not always go hand in hand. It is easy to forget that a strapping thirteen-year-old may not have the emotional or social sophistication that his appearance suggests and that he may be feeling as vulnerable and out of his depth as his smaller friends.

Early and late developers
There can be some advantages for boys who develop earlier than their friends. There is a certain amount of prestige in being bigger and stronger than your peers, and it can also help in terms of sporting prowess which often equates to popularity in adolescent males. In turn, this leads to greater self-esteem and assurance, which helps socially.

The downside of early development is that a twelve-year-old can easily look like a fifteen-year-old and parents and the public will have higher expectations of them. You may find yourself treating your towering son more like a grown-up and giving him more responsibility, but try to remember his age and that, in certain cases, he may only have the emotional maturity of a ten-year-old, despite his size.

A bigger problem for boys is late development. As your son watches his friends grow while he remains relatively small, he may become less confident, anxious or downright miserable. He is also at a disadvantage athletically and may be excluded from competition and team sports in favour of the more physically mature, stronger boys, thus adding to his sense of isolation and 'freakishness'.

Although his growth spurt may be very sudden (it is not unusual for a boy to gain as much as 12–15 cm (5–6 inches) in a year – that's a new pair of school trousers every term to you and me), puberty itself does not happen overnight. The onset is preceded by several years of hormonal adjustment as the pituitary gland at the base of the brain releases increasing

Nevertheless, doctors rarely recommend medical investigations on a short, pre-pubescent boy until he is fifteen at the earliest and, by that time, the damage to self-esteem can be done. What can parents do to minimize the effects of late development? You can boost self-esteem whenever possible and reassure him that the growth spurt will occur eventually. In fact, you might like to stress that late maturers have usually caught up by the age of eighteen and often end up taller than average. Another good morale booster is to tell him that boys are always taller than their mothers, which seems to be of some consolation.

However, do not be dismissive of his fears just because you know they are ungrounded. To him, this is a very real problem that he has to live with and even though he knows puberty will happen one fine day, it is not happening soon enough for his liking. You can only remain supportive and bide your time.

On a brighter note, a study has shown that late developing boys have a stronger sense of self and where they are going in life compared to their developed contemporaries, and they are less likely to experience the falling-off in academic achievement that often accompanies physical maturity when boys suddenly discover girls.

amounts of hormones to stimulate the gonads, or sex glands. In turn, once the gonads have released sufficient sex hormones, the sex organs will begin to develop and, hey presto, puberty is here.

This is a bewildering time for boys, but it is equally scary and confusing for parents. Suddenly your cuddly little boy starts to resemble his father rather too much for comfort. He no longer has that reassuring 'little boy' smell but instead gives off a whiff of something altogether more musty and unfamiliar. These changes in smell and feel are a direct result of the rising hormone levels and they may precede puberty itself by several years.

A faint suspicion that things are starting to change can be rather disconcerting and it may signal an alteration in your physical relationship with your son. Often, from the age of about eight or nine, boys seem less keen on cuddles and intimacy anyway and, if you have picked up on the subtle changes taking place in your son's body, you may find that you are happy to withdraw from too much physical contact. This is a great shame because at a time when boys may be struggling with bewildering changes in their emotions and their appearance, they need reassurance and the comfort of your touch should not be underestimated.

There's peer pressure to get into trouble. You get dared to do reckless things and it's chicken if you don't. But the stuff you do is calculated. You weigh up which dare you'll take and which you won't.

Eighteen-year-old

Body changes

The timing for the onset of puberty is governed by several factors: heredity, physical condition, nourishment, certain psychological influences, and individual variation.

The first sign of change is that the skin of the scrotum will darken as the testes begin to grow at about eleven to twelve years old. Don't worry if one testicle hangs lower than the other, this is quite common. If the testes have not started to enlarge by fourteen, then consult your doctor.

In early puberty, boys experience similar hormonal influences from oestrogen as girls, and as a result about 30 per cent of boys will develop slight breasts. Sometimes this swelling will only occur on one side and it feels more like a little lump than a budding breast, but don't be alarmed, it is really very common. These developments may last up to eighteen months before they disappear, but this can be a cause of great embarrassment while it lasts. Reassure your son that it is only temporary and it may be an idea to allow him to wear whichever clothes (usually baggy sportswear) make him feel less conspicuous and self-conscious until this stage passes.

At the same time (eleven to twelve years), your son will start to get some fine pubic hair and, if he has not already started feeling uncomfortable about undressing in front of you, do not be surprised if he starts to want some privacy now. Adolescents are intensely self-conscious of their changing bodies and are also very aware of others. If you have always wandered around the house naked and been relaxed about nudity, bear in mind that this could now be acutely embarrassing for your adolescent son. That does not mean that you should instantly cover up either, but consulting him

19

and acknowledging his discomfort might be a way to find what works best for you all.

Erections and wet dreams

At twelve to thirteen years, the penis starts to lengthen before it eventually thickens at the age of about fourteen, when erections will become more frequent.

Boys tend to spend a lot of time comparing the size of their penises. This is not strange or 'kinky' in any way, but natural curiosity and a compelling need to compare 'manhood'.

If your son feels that he is rather on the small side, you could-point out that although there is a lot of variation in the size of non-erect penises, these differences are ironed out once the penis is erect because smaller penises increase more in size than bigger ones. An average erect penis is between 12 and 17 cm (5 and 7 inches).

If he is open to discussion, you could also suggest that since he is looking at his penis from above, perspective makes it appear smaller than it really is. Get him to check it out in the mirror (like he needs telling!).

Most boys find that virtually anything can give them an erection at this time and it can be extremely embarrassing and inconvenient for them. The general consensus among dads and older boys interviewed for this book is that the best way to get an erection to subside is to concentrate very hard on something else.

About a year after the penis starts to lengthen, your son may have his first ejaculation. Initially, it will not contain sperm and will be a clear, sticky liquid; later, as the testicles start to produce sperm, it becomes milky in appearance.

> Mum and Dad told me all about sex and contraceptives and stuff, but they never mentioned anything about wet dreams and erections and all that, which would have been a lot more useful.
>
> *Sixteen-year-old*

The first ejaculation often happens during sleep and is commonly known as a 'wet' dream. Before you jump to the conclusion that your son is turning into a sex fiend, wet dreams are not necessarily a result of saucy dreams. Any sort of dreaming can trigger ejaculation and, since you dream shortly before waking up, it is a good idea to discreetly put a box of tissues on your son's bedside table in early adolescence. In this way, he can clean up and save himself and you some embarrassment and, more practically, he will not have to sleep on the wet patch.

Masturbation
First and foremost, let's clear up the myth that masturbation is harmful. If that were the case, about 90 per cent of the population would be at risk, and adolescent boys in particular.

At about the same time as your son gets his first erections, he will discover masturbation, and this is entirely natural and not to be discouraged. Of course, sex drive varies from individual to individual, but in the main, adolescent boys have sex on the mind frequently. They are easily aroused and there are stimuli all around them – from erotic advertising in magazines and on TV to their female classmates who are conspicuously emerging as young women. In order to cope with this frequent state of arousal, boys masturbate.

Experiencing the release and delight of orgasm without guilt is wonderfully liberating for him and it is a good first stepping stone on the road to sexual pleasure in partnered sex. Sons are rarely keen to share with their parents the news that they are now masturbating. However, you can give the tacit message that you do not disapprove by supplying tissues and requesting that they use these rather than routinely messing up bedding and pyjamas. Incidentally, a waste bin is not a bad idea either, as recommended by one mother who found a pile of used tissues under her son's bed several months after she had first supplied the tissue box.

Although most boys do not want to discuss this new-found pleasure in their lives, others take it completely in their stride. For instance, a good friend's thirteen-year-old son calmly asked her on the way home from school in the car, 'When did you start masturbating, Mum? Isn't it great!' You can judge her reaction by the skid marks on the road. Amazingly, she managed to mask her surprise and answered him to his satisfaction. Later, once she was over the shock, she realized how lucky she is that her son felt he could be that open with her.

If asked openly, you can let boys know that masturbation is okay and that you will respect the privacy of your son's bedroom after lights out. However, some young boys connect masturbation with pornography, and this is when you may feel you need to make your views known (see Chapter Four).

Incidentally, another myth that circulates among young lads is that if you have an erection, you have to ejaculate or it is painful or dangerous. If you get an opportunity, it is worth pointing out that this is simply not true. Tell your son that every erection subsides of its own accord eventually, whether he 'comes' or not. It may be uncomfortable for a while, but it is certainly not dangerous, and this myth should never be used to blackmail girls into having sex.

Other physical changes
Underarm, body and facial hair do not make an appearance until about thirteen to fifteen years, but hair growth varies greatly from boy to boy, and depends largely on family patterns. Hair on the stomach, chest and legs will continue to grow into early adulthood.

Unlike most developmental changes, the order of events in puberty may vary. Boys' growth spurts typically lags two or so years behind the girls who begin at about eleven. Boys tend to start to shoot up at about thirteen, grow fastest at fourteen, and then slow down at sixteen. At around the same time as he shoots up, your son will also start to beef up – he will put on weight and muscle and his shoulders will broaden. At the beginning of puberty, only about 17–20 per cent of body weight in boys is fat, and this drops to about 10–12 per cent by seventeen. Teenage boys remain lighter than men and continue to broaden out until they are about twenty-five years old.

You may find that your son becomes uncharacteristically clumsy during puberty, and it may help to temper your exasperation over 'accidents' and spillages in the home if you realize that there is a physiological reason for this. During the adolescent growth spurt, the lower parts of the limbs grow first, i.e. feet and hands lengthen, then calf and forearm and then thigh and upper arm followed by the hips, chest and shoulders.

At first, the bones of the limbs are growing at almost twice the speed as those of the trunk, thus giving adolescents that distinctive gangly, Neanderthal look. It can also result in temporary clumsiness, which is as puzzling and infuriating for him as it is for you – tolerance is the watchword here.

As his body matures and grows at breakneck speed, so good sleep is essential because it is during your son's slumber that the pubertal and growth hormones are secreted. You may notice that your son is going to bed later and later, but he is no longer getting up at the crack of dawn either. Actually, a crowbar may be necessary to prise him from his bed in

Growing pains

'Growing pains' are common in early adolescents, but the cause is not known. They are experienced as cramp-like pains deep in the muscles of the legs, away from the joints. They are usually felt late in the afternoon or at night and often after a day of high activity, although this is not the cause.

Attacks can last from between a few minutes to an hour. You can try heat or massage to relieve the discomfort. Growing pains can continue for several years and whereas you should reassure your son that they are not serious, it is worth getting him checked out by your GP to eliminate any serious skeletal disorder.

the mornings. Recent research from the US shows that, far from being a sign of laziness, this common teenage trait has a physiological root. Brain chemistry does not allow teenagers to fall to sleep much before 11.30 p.m. and yet, unlike mature adults, they still need the full eight to ten hours' sleep in order to grow. If you rouse them from their slumber early in the morning, they will perform like zombies. In the US, trials that allowed teenagers to start school at a later hour than the customary 8.00 a.m. showed a marked improvement in teenagers' school work.

You will probably also notice around this time that he is no longer bursting with energy from the minute he gets up to the minute he goes to bed as he was when he was younger – every cloud has a silver lining!

Voice changes
As the larynx grows larger, so the voice starts to deepen. This happens in both sexes but it is more pronounced in boys. Usually the process happens over some time and there will be an uneasy period during which an adolescent has to endure unexpected and mortifying squeaks when he talks. Unfortunately, he has no control over the pitch of his voice as the larynx gradually enlarges and forms the typically male, prominent Adam's apple. Occasionally, the voice breaks very suddenly – seemingly overnight – and without warning your son will address you in a new, deeper voice. This, of course, may come as quite a shock, but it does have the merit that he is saved the embarrassment of an unreliable speaking voice.

Testosterone

As they grow, boys experience several growth spurts and energy surges associated with high levels of testosterone. At about the age of four, his testosterone level almost doubles but then calms down again at about five when it drops by half. Between eleven and thirteen years, levels rise sharply again causing a sudden growth spurt. This testosterone boost takes levels to 800 per cent higher than those of a toddler. A male's testosterone peak is at about 14.

Voice changes are something of a lottery (in fact, some voices never deepen, a condition known as puberphonia), and there are no guarantees that a good boy singer will have a good adult voice. On the other hand, the adult voice may be much improved, so fingers crossed.

What's that smell

At puberty, the apocrine (sweat) glands in the armpits and around the genitals start to work, producing sweat when the body is hot or when a person is nervous or excited – a frequent state for many adolescents. Fresh sweat does not smell, but if left for a couple of days, it will. If your son has not already got the cleanliness bug that so many youngsters catch, it is a

Parents seem to think it's all a big joke. They don't realize how embarrassing it can be when your voice lets you down. *Fifteen-year-old*

Spots and acne

Acne is the blight of teenagers and something that both sexes dread. It is often worse in boys due to their greasier skins, caused by higher levels of testosterone. It is most common between the ages of sixteen and nineteen and, despite the myths, there is no scientific evidence that junk food, chocolate, dairy products or fried foods cause spots.

Emotional stress and tiredness, on the other hand, can trigger spots in certain prone teenagers and this is one to watch. Many teenagers report that their skin condition improves over the summer when they are in the fresh air more often, and sunlight certainly seems to help.

Cleansing the skin thoroughly, but not excessively, is the best way to prevent and deal with spots and, despite the satisfaction it gives, squeezing spots should be avoided since this simply makes them more inflamed.

For most adolescent boys, spots are just one more cause for anxiety and embarrassment, but in some cases severe acne can make a boy's life a misery. Taunts along the lines of 'pizza face' can seriously undermine his self-confidence. If the spots are bad and continue for some time, you should consult a doctor who can prescribe systemic antibiotics and topical preparations, which may improve the condition.

At-a-glance puberty physical development chart

Age	Development
11–12	Fine, straight pubic hair forms at base of penis.
12–13	Testicles enlarge; skin of scrotum darkens.
	Possible development of slight breasts.
	Growth spurt begins.
13–15	Penis starts to lengthen, eventually thickening a year or so later.
	First ejaculation usually begins about a year after penis begins to lengthen.
	Pubic hair gets coarser and curls.
	Underarm, body and facial hair starts to develop
	Underarm sweat glands develop together with an adult body odour.
	Larynx enlarges causing Adam's apple to become more prominent.
14–15	The voice starts to deepen.
16–17	End of growth spurt.
	Hair growth on abdomen, chest and legs continues into adulthood.
17–18	Sexual maturity reached.

kindness to point out that he needs to wash his armpits and genital area every day and probably use an underarm deodorant. You may find it embarrassing to raise the subject with your son, but teenagers can be very cruel to anyone who whiffs of BO (body odour). Therefore, when you are struggling with embarrassment, hold on to the thought that it's kinder coming from you than from them.

■ PROBLEM SOLVING

My son has turned into a couch potato

Anyone who is familiar with the Harry Enfield characters, Kevin and Perry, will know that adolescent boys can make doing nothing an art form. Having spent the past fourteen years trying to tire out your boisterous boy, you are now faced with exactly the opposite problem, i.e. how to get him to do anything. It can be infuriating when you speak to your teenage son who is draped across the armchair like a languid sloth, only to be met on the third repetition with a distracted, 'Wha d'ya say?' You begin to wonder how your previously bright boy can be so vacant.

Wonder no more. It is because behind that blank expression, his mind is preoccupied with thoughts of his new-found sexuality, how to use it and what the future holds. Beneath his inane mask his mind is whirring, but he only thinks about the things that matter to him – anything else is just an annoyance.

As for you, you are a bit of a nuisance too, as far as he is concerned. He's working hard at doing nothing and you are messing things up by asking him to do something. His home life is devoted to loafing in bed, lying around listening to his music or vegging in front of the television – this is adolescent boy heaven. Teenage boys, in particular, are very good at doing nothing in comfort and style. So, is there an answer? Well, you're not going to change this typically teenage behaviour because young boys enjoy it too much, but you can lessen its irritating effects.

What you can do

- Always start from the premise that effort is anathema to your son and, therefore, whatever you ask will be met with surly complaint or an excuse for why someone else should do it. Be firm.
- Remember that this inertia is reserved principally for his own home. At school or socializing with friends he can still be the live wire he always has been.
- Look out for the teenage boy tactic of saying 'yes' to a request to do something in order to avoid a fight, and then sloping off to his room (or somewhere quiet) without actually doing or completing the task. Stay vigilant and make him finish what he started.
- Do not give up and do it yourself – if monitored, he will begrudgingly do what you ask but, realistically, he will instantly revert to his lethargy as soon as the job is over.
- Cereal packets wide open on the counter, coke cans left next to the armchair, dirty plate and open jam pot next to the toaster – this is the detritus of teenage life. Try to instil the principle of clearing up after himself but resign yourself to the fact that you probably will have to keep reminding him and do not get too steamed up about it.
- Hold on to the thought that this phase does pass – he has not permanently lost the use of his gross motor skills. By seventeen or eighteen, he may even laughingly admit what a pain he was a few years back!

■ **CASE STUDY – Susie's story**

The physical changes in your son's appearance brought about by puberty are very dramatic and yet they may creep up on you, as one mum explains.

'As a mum, you make all the jokes about spotting the one solitary, sprouting pubic hair on your adolescent son but, in reality, it all goes on behind closed doors and you're scarcely aware of the changes until there's this fully formed man in your midst. It's really quite bizarre.

'I suppose because it happens over a period of time, you're not so aware of each development as it occurs. I guess the thing that struck me was that one day, I telephoned home and a man answered and I remember thinking, "Who's that?" and then realizing it was my son, Matt.

'I guess I knew his voice was breaking but it hadn't really dawned on me until then. You only noticed the occasional wobble and a squeak when he was trying to talk very loudly. He might well have been embarrassed when it let him down but he never spoke of it.

'There's a tacit understanding that things are going on behind closed bedroom doors but you don't pry. It's like every mother can spot a normal dirty, smelly sock on the floor so you soon realize when a discarded sock has been used for something other than footwear. At the time, I was surprised to find out that a few other mums had had the same "sticky sock" experience and we all decided it was high time to put a toilet roll next to his bed, if you get my drift. That's what I mean about tacit understandings.

'Otherwise, both my older sons have been remarkably discreet about puberty. Spending a lot of time in their rooms is part of being a teenager and becoming more private about their bodies dovetails nicely with that. Without making any sort of conscious decision, I don't think I ever saw them undressed from about the age of eleven.

'My youngest boy is thirteen now and eager for it all to happen. I haven't detected any physical changes yet but perhaps I'll be more conscious of it with my last. He wants to start shaving like his brothers but he's still only got down on his cheeks.

'Oh yes, that was another thing. I remember going on holiday and seeing Luke in shorts and being surprised that he had hairy legs. For some reason, that really threw me. But, in general, the changes just creep up on you and nobody makes a song and dance about it – least of all the kids.'

3

Puberty and the way he feels

Although the physical changes of puberty are very dramatic and hard to ignore, it is the emotional and intellectual developments of adolescence that are perhaps the most profound.

This is the stage of child-rearing that many parents dread. You hear horror stories of difficult teenagers causing constant fights and disharmony, and shudder at the thought of the turbulent and chaotic period in family life that awaits you. In reality, although this undoubtedly happens in some homes, for many parents this is a time when you can enjoy your children's growing understanding and independence, and can be proud of their achievements. Despite the media scare-mongering, most teenage boys move smoothly away from their parents' control into a life of independence with only minor family skirmishes along the way.

There will of course be a few ups and downs associated with the transition through the many new phases of adolescence, but nothing that is insurmountable given a sensible approach, a sense of humour and a large dose of goodwill and patience. It seems that young people tend to deal with the

> There were times when I liked my parents during
> puberty.   *Eighteen-year-old*

challenge of each new aspect of adolescence as it arises and,
as parents, we should take a leaf out of their book.

During a time of rapid change, it is wise to work on the
assumption that you can cross each bridge as you come to
it. Do not fall into the trap of assuming that an unpleasant
incident will necessarily escalate or of believing that one row
is the start of permanent bad relations between you and your
son. Instead, look forward to this exciting new phase in your
child's life, offer practical help towards achieving independence where possible, and continue to show that you care at
every opportunity.

Emotional change
For boys, puberty brings with it an overwhelming desire
for challenge and independence. Surging hormones
make them want to seek adventure and glory and thrills
and spills as they burgeon their way into manhood. On
the one hand, they want to stretch their wings and do
their own thing, yet, on the other, they want desperately to fit in with their peer group and to be cool. This
dilemma dominates the period surrounding puberty and
boys' conflicting emotions, anxieties and self-doubts
usually manifest themselves in challenging behaviour
for parents.

Yet, despite everything that they say and do to the contrary, this is a time when your son desperately needs your
love, guidance and support.

No one said it was going to be easy but if you can, consider that, just like infancy where you looked forward to each developmental milestone, adolescence passes through distinct phases. Realizing that each new development is transitory can help you to deal with it more positively.

Certainly there is no point in beating yourself up with the 'Where did I go wrong?' style of questioning. Although it is a common and perfectly natural reaction when your hitherto charming son becomes alternately rude, selfish, defiant or surly, the smell of burning martyr cuts no ice with teenagers. A self-reproachful attitude only results in making you feel like a failure. It is far more productive to alter your approach and to ask yourself 'What am I doing/what can I do right?' Hold on to the thought that this challenging behaviour will not outlast adolescence.

Of course, you do not have to like it or even put up with it, but do not worry yourself unnecessarily that this is your son's character set in stone for eternity. Rather, recognize the main emotional and intellectual milestones as they arise, breathe a sigh of relief as they pass and look forward to the wonderful, mature man that is going to emerge at the end.

In the meantime, here are some of the more common developmental stages to forearm you. Then we shall progress to tactics for dealing with them, as recommended by the battle-scarred parents who have been through it all before.

What to look out for
There are three distinct phases of adolescence and each brings with it its own and uniquely challenging set of behaviours. The period of adolescence spans the years between

puberty and eighteen, the age of legal adulthood. It is roughly broken down into early (age eleven to fourteen), middle (age fifteen to sixteen) and late (age seventeen to eighteen) adolescence.

The following list represents the general patterns of behaviour that can develop during each of the three stages. Your son may exhibit some or all of these developments, depending on how lucky or unlucky you are. The ages given are a rough guideline only – each boy matures at his own pace. However, at least if you know roughly what to expect and when, you can be prepared and, hopefully, respond in a more positive way.

Behaviour milestones for early adolescents
(eleven to fourteen years)

- *Self-conscious about appearance*. Irritating though this obsession may be, recognize that it is useless to try to convince a teenager that appearances do not matter. At this stage, their self-esteem is irrevocably linked to friendship and they are not yet secure enough to believe that their friends like them for themselves. They know that appearances play a large part in how friends judge each other.
- *Surliness.* This is a result of hormonal changes and even the most easy-going, gentle boys can become uncharacteristically aggressive and rude at this time.
- *Rudeness.* In surveys, this comes top of the list of parents' grumbles about adolescents.

- *Experiments with dress, speech, manners, etc.* These are all an attempt to assert his own identity and to move on from being 'just one of the family'.
- *Wants more independence.* It is a fine line between giving greater licence and overprotecting our children, but be prepared for increased demands for more freedom.
- *Over-inflamed sense of injustice.* You will probably be sick of the phrase, 'It is not fair' by the end of this phase, particularly since issues are often viewed solely from his own viewpoint and in black and white. This development often leads to increased friction between siblings (see pages 50–3) and even to clashes with school or other authorities.
- *Friends take on great importance*. Wearing the right clothes, listening to the same music, and using the same slang are all symptoms of the need to be accepted by the peer group. Be warned – your son may start to hold up friends and their parents as a yardstick and be critical of you as parents.

Behaviour milestones for middle adolescents (fifteen to sixteen years)
- *Self-consciousness diminishes.* Once again, your son becomes less shy and more sociable. Who knows, he may even agree to socialize with your friends.

In puberty, if your parents impose restrictions, you do it ten times worse.   *Twenty-year-old*

- **Better able to compromise and to be less self-absorbed.** The overall effect is that your son is easier to live with again as he begins to accept that others' opinions and viewpoints may have some validity, even if they differ from his own.
- **Friends are less influential.** As he learns to think more independently, your son is less keen to conform. He becomes more discriminating and is less suggestible. The downside of this development is that he is also more likely to resist your efforts to interfere in or control his life.
- **Seeks new experiences and takes risks.** Often manifested by experimentation with alcohol, cigarettes and soft drugs, and a desire to test boundaries.
- **Develops own sense of morality and values.** He may question or reject your family values in favour of his own.
- **Exploring sexuality.** He may start dating or form a sexual relationship, but could become rather secretive about his experiences and feelings (see Chapter Four).
- **Forms deep and lasting friendships.** It is the start of the 'You treat this house like a hotel' phase as he chooses to spend more time with friends and less time at home.
- **Develops wider interests, broader intellect and greater interest in the world at large.** Be prepared to discuss and debate issues at length,
- **Specializations appear.** A strong interest in something creative, such as art or music, may emerge and strengths in specific school subjects will come to the fore.
- **Risk taking.** He will become more physically and socially adventurous and may want to take up daring sports such as rock climbing or want to travel independently.

- **Gets on better with mother than father.** A survey shows that by seventeen and eighteen, nearly one-third of boys are getting on 'badly' with their dads.

Behaviour milestones for late adolescents (seventeen to eighteen)

- **Starts to form stable sexual relationships.** This is when the first serious girlfriend may appear on the scene and he becomes sure of his sexual orientation.
- **Strives for complete independence.** The anxiety and effort involved in trying to achieve financial and emotional independence can result in bursts of temper and crises of confidence.
- **Wants equality as an adult.** He wants to be treated as an equal but tends to feel that he has more insight into the world than his tired old parents, which can be irritating in the extreme.
- **Social and/or political awareness.** Idealism often leads young men to support social or political causes or to explore religious movements.
- **Greater involvement with the world at large.** He will probably want to spend more time with friends or work colleagues and may not want to come on a family holiday any more.
- **Self-reliance.** He may be ready to fly the nest and find a place of his own.

What your son is experiencing

Puberty marks a leap in your son's cognitive development that makes him more aware of himself and his place in the group. It is a time when competition consumes young adolescent

In with the in-crowd

Despite the *Lord of the Flies* culture that flourishes among adolescent boys, provided that your son is not a complete oddity, he stands a good chance of enjoying a large gang of friends. Unlike girls who tend to be cliquey at this age, boys like to 'hang out' with a wide, loose circle of mates.

Although during pre-puberty, being good at sport and being tough are the most highly valued qualities, just being fun or good company is also a passport to social acceptance among older boys.

And even if he can't be cool and doesn't quite fit in, it is not so terrible for boys, because boys do not get so hung up about social status or ostracism as girls. As far as the stylishly-challenged are concerned, there are plenty of other geeky lads to hang around with. Many boys just do not care about being cool or having style and they are perfectly happy as they are. They have their small circle of friends who enjoy the same interests and, for the most part, the other boys leave them to their own devices. In this sense, boys have it easier than girls during adolescence.

males. They are constantly assessing who is best at every activity, from sporting prowess through academic achievement to success with girls. And each boy is acutely aware of his placing in the pecking order.

It is a time when his heightened self-awareness prompts your son to want to conform to his friends. Male adolescence is a fairly cruel environment in which he is held up to ridicule for the slightest diversion from what is considered the norm. This could be the wrong haircut, liking the wrong music, wearing the wrong brand of trainers, even down to having some physical 'defect' such as freckles or red hair. Whatever it is, it singles him out for derision. Yet these rules that he transgresses at his peril are not written down – he must perceive them as he goes along and woe betide him if he is slow on the uptake. Your son will tell you that it is just light-hearted teasing but for the boy who is perpetually at the wrong end of the ribbing, it can be a painful process.

Within their group of friends or with other kids generally, adolescent boys constantly make pre-emptive strikes to divert attention from themselves and onto others. They live in fear that at any moment the glare of scorn could be turned on them and so verbally they lash out first. The unending quest to fit in, to be cool, pits boys against one another, and part of proving yourself is to belittle others.

Parents as the enemy
The overwhelming need to 'fit in' with his peer group coincides with a hormonally driven desire to cut loose from parental control and influences. It is an irresistible urge towards independence that is essential if your son is to grow into a self-reliant adult.

Unfortunately, this urge to turn away from childhood usually manifests itself with a sudden aversion to you, his parents. Even a perfectly innocent enquiry about what sort of a day he has had can be met by revulsion. Your son now wants to get away from you as soon as possible. For many an adolescent boy, his bedroom becomes his sanctuary.

> The idea of your parents helping you through puberty
> is a misnomer. The only way they can help is by going
> away and letting you party.   *Eighteen-year-old*

After stocking up on food and drink, he will retire to his room, turn his music up loud and that will be the last you see of him. Not literally, of course, but for the early years of adolescence, your son may well lock himself away for an inordinate amount of time.

While he is getting to grips with his sexuality, he will be intensely private and resent any intrusions by his parents. At this time, he would rather keep himself separate.

Sadly though, the combination of needing to look cool among friends and shutting out his parents means that many young boys experience a sense of isolation. They are hurting from the cruel teasing and taunting banter that characterizes early male adolescence and yet they are unable to discuss it with loved ones for fear of losing face and because they feel the need to be separate.

In the *Leading Lads* survey, fewer than half said that they were likely to turn to a friend if they had a problem or felt depressed. 'My mates would think I was pathetic,' they explained, reflecting the feeling that to open up to friends would show vulnerability and thus make you an open target for contempt. As they reach late adolescence, this sad situation appears to improve and our own findings suggest that boys do confide in one or two very close teenage friends, but only once trust has been gained and proven.

> In certain ways, male friends overtly contribute less but actually, on a deeper level, contribute a lot more and last for life really.   *Twenty-year-old*

It seems that some young men are able to turn to their family or other caring adults for emotional backup, usually choosing mothers first. However, for many, barriers stand in the way of getting any help.

Boys often believe that to act like a man 'is to stand on your own two feet and shoulder your own problems'. If the role-model image they have latched onto has been an illusory superhero, as depicted on screen and in books, they will equate manliness with strength and stoicism and they, in turn, will feel the need to suffer in silence.

Sadly, this belief led to a number of young men bottling up their problems until they became unbearable. They described how they learned to keep it to themselves. If fathers were silent on the subject of feelings or relationships, sons felt that this was how a man should behave. Among extremely depressed young men, over half believed that 'Boys must be tough to survive', and 'Boys are expected to match up to one ideal of maleness, and cope with problems themselves,' states Adrienne Katz in the *Leading Lads* report.

Young men also hold the misguided view that it is 'manly' to protect parents from their problems 'because they've got so much on their plate right now'. A common reaction amongst boys was to feel that they could not burden their parents with their own problems when they know their parents are under stress. This mistaken altruism is a sign that your son pos-

> Parents are the enemy at puberty. They embarrass
> you in public just by being alive. *Eighteen-year-old*

sesses the wonderful male traits of loyalty and a desire to
protect, but it is important that parents make it clear that they
are strong enough to handle whatever their son needs to talk
about.

At puberty, boys are particularly prone to the pressure to
appear masculine, which roughly translated in a young adolescent boy's mind means anything that is not feminine. If
they equate traits such as empathy, tenderness, and shows of
emotion as feminine qualities, they will detest these features
in each other and will be at pains to make sure that they do
not exhibit any of these qualities.

Self-confidence
Between the ages of ten and fourteen, boys feel most vulnerable about their size, strength, performance, and their developing sexuality. However, between eleven and thirteen, their
fear of homosexuality reaches epic proportions. They do not
understand their sexuality clearly yet and they are not secure
enough to know that any taunts about being homosexual are
not founded in some element of truth (see page 72). Such is
the fear of being gay, and thus different, it becomes the worst
insult a thirteen-year-old can hurl at someone.

Puberty is a time of great change and moments of transition are scary for anyone, but some youngsters seem especially vulnerable as they pass through this huge life transformation. Even the most 'together' boy will have the odd blow

> The lower profile you can keep, the higher respect
> your kids will keep you in.   *Sixteen-year-old*

struck at his self-esteem and all will experience peaks and troughs in their confidence throughout the teenage years.

Your son will measure himself against a new yardstick as he enters adolescence, and although there will inevitably be the odd dip in self-esteem, if handled sensitively his confidence should grow throughout the teenage years as he meets and overcomes new challenges and becomes more independent. Problems in self-esteem seem to arise when he has too much to cope with at once or if the changes come too suddenly. If he is just managing to cope with his self-consciousness about his changing body, but also has stress at home, problems in school, and conflicts with friends, then his self-esteem will take a knock. It seems that most teenagers ride the turmoil of adolescence pretty well but they find it easier to do so if they can take problems one at a time.

The emotional support from caring adults is essential at this time, despite any protestations to the contrary, but there are a few other parental contributions that can help your sons through the emotional minefield that is puberty.

What you can do
Ironically, puberty is a time characterized by both parent and child feeling as if they cannot do anything right. In fact, there is much that you can do to help your son pass through adolescence with his self-esteem intact, and to make life for the whole family more civilized and less fraught.

- **Boost your son's self-esteem whenever possible.**
  You learn to value yourself if others show that they
  value you. If you praise your son's achievements and
  encourage him to make decisions, he will pick up positive messages that boost his confidence. Most parents have simply no idea how much their opinion is
  valued by their children.
- **Tell him that you love him.** It is easy to assume that
  your children know they are loved and that it does not
  need stating, yet many young lads doubt their worth
  and need their parents to reiterate this.
- **Listen to your son and be supportive and understanding.** Being loving is a great foundation, but
  the *Leading Lads* survey suggests that 75 per cent
  of boys with the highest life satisfaction scores had
  parents who also 'listen to my problems and my
  views'.
- **Allow him to develop his own values and to
  express them.** By doing this, if your son comes under
  pressure from friends to do something he is not comfortable with, he will have the confidence to speak out.
- **Do not be critical.** You may think that the things
  you are criticizing are only trivial, such as their
  clothes or choice of music, but it matters to boys
  and, hard though it may be to believe, so does your
  good opinion.
- **If you criticize, try to be positive.** Phrase your comments to save their feelings where possible. Despite a
  cocky exterior, teenagers are easily hurt.
- **Be conscious of adolescent insecurity.** Even if you
  are simply joshing, teenagers are extremely sensitive,

especially about personal appearance or feelings. Sarcasm, in particular, can be very destructive.

- **Separate the behaviour from the person.** If you dislike their behaviour, make sure that they understand that it is the conduct and not them you dislike.
- **Help them to find areas of expertise.** Self-esteem grows with success. It is unhelpful if your son constantly finds himself in situations where he is almost bound to fail.
- **Trust their judgement.** They will be more confident about making decisions given the right encouragement and guidance from you.
- **Accept them for who they are.** Your son is an individual who may not have the same likes or dislikes and interests as you. He may not fulfil the ambition you long for, but it is important that you let him know that you are happy with him just the way he is.
- **Avoid 'labelling' him.** It can take many years to shake off the identity that you have been given by the family, so be cautious before you start calling him 'clumsy' or 'dopey' or 'the quiet one'.
- **Do not compare one child with another.** See sibling rivalry, page 50.
- **Talk as a family as much as possible.** If a teenager is in a family that talks to each other and expresses feelings openly, he will feel more confident about trying to explain how he feels and why he acts as he does.

Finally, it is a common belief among adults that teenagers are too cocky for their own good. How many times have you heard someone say, 'He needs cutting down to size' or 'He's getting too big for his boots'? However, adults often forget that in the majority of cases this is mere bravado – a thinly veiled attempt to convince the world at large that the adolescent is more confident than he really feels.

The temptation – and it is very real – to cut him down to size should be resisted. Your son needs to feel good about himself if he is to do well socially and in school. High self-esteem gives him a sense that he is somehow doing something right in his life. If you pull him down a peg or two whenever he starts to swagger, you will give him the impression, rightly or wrongly, that you do not greatly value your son and he will soon cease to feel good about himself. It is far better to explain the effect that ill-considered, big talk has on you and on others – you may be surprised at how he takes this on board.

When the going gets tough

You may think that you would have to be a saint to be able to do all of the above when faced with a surly, non-communicative, ungrateful thirteen-year-old, but it is surprising how implementing even a few of these suggestions can make a difference to your son's behaviour.

No one can get it right all of the time though, so do not set your expectations too high. Simply bear in mind the theory – it is compiled from experts' and parents' experiences – and put it into practice when you feel up to it.

Nevertheless, if despite all your best efforts your son's behaviour is really getting you down and you feel used and abused, go easy on yourself. Take a bit of time out and indulge in activities that give you a sense of well-being and fulfilment (see Chapter Twelve).

However, no matter how troublesome your son is being, never be tempted to withdraw affection. Dr Terri Apter, social psychologist and Senior Tutor at Newnham College, Cambridge, showed in a study that parents often pull back from their children in response to their apparent desire for independence at a time when their children really need them. This left the teenagers feeling emotionally rejected and alone, and it is a common cause of distress between parents and teenagers.

That does not mean that you cannot let your son know how much you dislike his behaviour. However, be careful to also let him know that you still care about him. It is generally accepted that you need tolerance to live with a teenager and you may find that, for a peaceful life, you turn a blind eye quite often. Yet, experts agree that adolescents need and want to know just how far they can go. Imposing sensible limits and fair rules counted high on the list of good parenting skills in the *Leading Lads* survey of 1,400 boys. Naturally, your son may protest loudly and challenge you on every issue but, when push comes to shove, 70 per cent of boys with high self-esteem in the survey said that 'my parents lay down the right rules'.

What you can do
Coping during fraught times requires a good sense of humour, a sense of proportion, and a good support network of sympathetic friends and family. To make things easier on yourself, you should also take heed of the following recommendations from our panel of seasoned campaigners – the parents interviewed for this book:

- **Decide what is important to you.** Of course you have to set limits, but you could find yourself battling over every little thing. Some things matter more than others – obviously where safety is involved or where the behaviour is intolerable to the rest of the family – but let some things go rather than face constant conflict.

- **Be realistic.** If you swear like a trouper when driving, drink like a fish on a Saturday night and smoke like a chimney, it is hard to impose a blanket ban on cursing, drinking and smoking on your teenage son, and still keep your credibility intact. Limiting their consumption would be more realistic.

- **Do not be afraid to change your mind.** It is not weak to alter your position on something. On the contrary, it shows your children that if they can persuade you convincingly, as opposed to wearing you down by nagging, you are prepared to take their reasoned arguments into consideration.

- **Do not be nagged or bullied into submission.** Changing your mind because of sensible persuasion is not the same as being badgered into something. If your teenage son gets his own way simply by wearing you down, he has a good incentive to continue with this line of behaviour.

Sibling tensions

From between the ages of about eleven to fourteen, friction between siblings seems to be at its worst. From our interviews, either constant bickering or, where two boys were involved, the awfulness and brutality of their physical fights were reported as one of the biggest causes of upset to parents of teenagers.

Siblings who have hitherto enjoyed a good relationship may, as adolescents, be at each other's throats much of the time. Your privacy-loving adolescent probably resents a younger brother or sister 'interfering' in his life. So, when your thirteen-year-old inevitably overreacts to some minor incursion, the younger sibling sits smugly by, enjoying the ensuing argument while mum or dad wades in to sort out the fracas. Sound familiar?

If this scene is played out often enough – and it probably will be – the teenager will feel that he is drawing a disproportionate amount of parental fire or, in teenage parlance, you are playing favourites.

Yet, the problem with ignoring sibling fights when your sons are teenagers is that the stakes are so much higher. Teenagers are bigger and stronger, and can and do injure each other if they fight. When it comes to physical violence, you cannot stand back and let them sort it out for themselves in case one of them ends up seriously hurt. You must make it clear that you cannot and will not tolerate any behaviour that could result in injury. Your partner has an important role to play in backing you up on this one.

According to Professor Juliet Mitchell, a leading British psychoanalyst, Freud's theory that parent-child relationships harbour unconscious conflicts that can torment us for a lifetime has a vital missing element: it seems that siblings can screw up your psyche too. Mitchell believes that being superseded in your parents' affections by a new baby can have profound consequences, and that these can have repercussions in later 'lateral' relationships, such as marriage and partnerships or with work colleagues. She says, 'I would argue that the adolescent experience repeats the earlier childhood one. A three-year-old with a new sibling is in despair and oscillating between extreme love and hate but it's usually manageable – a sixteen-year-old with a thirteen-year-old is harder because the violence that is involved can be actually dangerous ...'

With the exception of violent fights, the same rules for dealing with sibling battles apply whatever your children's ages.

What you can do
It takes the diplomacy of a hostage negotiator to sort out sibling quarrels, but here are some suggestions garnered from other parents and experts:

- *Never take sides.* It is rare to get to the bottom of who started it, so stay impartial. Once you are involved the issue is forgotten and it now becomes a contest for parental favour – the original problem has been superseded.
- *Do not play judge and jury.* If you enter into a debate with each child pleading his case, it will go on for ever.
- *Do not shout.* If you join in the slanging match, the row will simply escalate.
- *Do not always blame the adolescent.* Just because he is older it does not mean that he is always at fault when he quarrels with a younger sibling. It is tempting to believe that he is to blame because you tend to protect the youngest.
- *Help them to resolve their own disputes.* Playing a mediating role without getting too involved or angry

can help both parties to explain how they feel and what this is really about.

- *Do not compare one child to another.* You will only cause resentments and jealousy if you appear to value one child's qualities and achievements above those of another.
- *Check that it is not always the same child you blame.* If one child is being singled out as the cause of all the trouble and the root of all evils in your household, you either have a troubled child or a family scapegoat. In reality, each member of a household causes their fair share of trouble, thus if one is always being picked on, you need to discover why. Sometimes a child becomes a scapegoat if they do not quite fit the family image or ideal.

■ PROBLEM SOLVING

My son takes me for granted

Let's not beat about the bush – adolescents are self-absorbed, self-centred and selfish (that's enough selfs to be getting on with). But, thankfully, not in every aspect of their lives. When it comes to adopting a dolphin, animal hospital, environmental issues, world injustice or a friend in need, your teenage son will be a picture of concern, even altruism.

It is a sad fact of life that it is you, his parents, for whom most of his selfish behaviour is reserved and, although it does not make it any more bearable, that is largely because you have done a good job. Despite the appearance of sophistication and his 'grown-up' body, your son is not yet an adult and he still counts on your unconditional love and support. He simply does not see that he is treating you badly and taking your kindness and good-natured help for granted. He will though. Once he reaches late adolescence (seventeen to eighteen years), he may even admit that he was hell to live with and that he treated you abysmally but, until then, here are some stopgaps to keep your sanity.

What you can do

- *Challenge selfish behaviour.* Let him know when he is being inconsiderate.
- *Don't be pushed around.* Your natural desire to please your kids means that you may end up doing more than you really want to and, sad to say, your son will put on you as often as you are prepared to put up with it. Learn to say 'No' once in a while.
- *Remember that this is 'normal' teenage behaviour.* His behaviour may be objectionable, but your son is not a monster just because he treats you so shabbily. In his mind, it is because you are 'just my parents'. In all probability, he is not the least bit selfish with other people.
- *It will pass.* This is a developmental stage – it is unpleasant while it lasts, but it will pass.

■ **CASE STUDY – Robert's story**

Despite the fact that all parents know there will come a time when your son is embarrassed by you, when it actually happens it can be more painful than you might expect, as one father explains.

'Like all parents we'd made the jokes about how our kids would be mortified if we started dancing at a school disco etc., but it really came as a shock when I realized that Mark found me an embarrassment full stop.

'Since he started at secondary school, I've always taken him to school in the mornings because it's on my way to work. I used to drop him off outside the gates, but when he was in Year 8, he told me to start dropping him off around the corner. I put it down to the fact that he didn't want his mates to realize he had a lift to school.

'But one day, I happened to be in the area at "going home" time. It was tipping down with rain so I pulled up at the bus stop and offered Mark and his mates a lift home. He was furious. The others hopped in and I thought for a moment that Mark was going to stay in the rain but he finally got in and sat in silence all the way home. Later, he told me that he'd never been so embarrassed and that I was never, under any circumstances, to ever do a thing like that again.

'I really was shocked. I thought I was doing him a favour. I hadn't realized that just being seen with his dad was embarrassing enough but mixing with his friends was an absolute cardinal sin.

'What really rubbed salt in the wound is that Mark seemed to actively like his friend Daniel's dad, Peter. He was forever quoting Peter as if he was the font of all knowledge and yet he wouldn't believe a word I said. I could say the self same thing as Peter but it would be greeted with snorts of derision whereas, if Peter said it, he'd probably take his advice and think it was gospel.

'I know there's a certain amount of growing away from the home during adolescence, but I have to admit I found this rejection a bit hurtful. Despite all the joking, when it happens to you and you realize that your kids are ashamed of you, it's not very nice.

'My wife, Sarah, said not to take it personally and not to let it stand between me and Mark, but it was difficult. I felt like retaliating on occasions. I felt belittled. I nearly made him get the bus in the morning like every other bugger but I resisted – what good would that do? Mark didn't seem to realize at all. It was as if he was blissfully unaware that he'd upset me.

'I think it was probably two or three years before Mark ceased to see Sarah and me as an embarrassment. Until then, he hated it if either of us tried to make conversation with his friends or anything like that. But when he was about sixteen or seventeen, he seemed to come out of it. I remember going to his friend's brother's eighteenth birthday party and we all had a great time. I think I may have even danced, much to Mark's mock horror, but it was actually very good-natured teasing, I recall.

'I'm glad now that I didn't react badly at the time, but it was very tempting. We'd always been so close and loving that nothing had prepared me for Mark's obvious embarrassment at being seen with his parents.'

4

Discovering sexuality

It can be hard for parents to face up to a child's awakening sexuality. For many, it is a sign of his growing independence and the first stark realization that there is part of his life that is separate from you and your protection.

From the first stirrings of sexual awareness to full sexual relationships will, of course, take some time but, in Western societies, sexual activity is taking place at an earlier and earlier age. In the US, statistics show that 50 per cent of fifteen- to seventeen-year-old boys are sexually experienced and in Britain the figure rises to 74 per cent by eighteen-years-old.

As we saw in Chapter Three, puberty can start as young as nine years old, although more commonly it is around eleven years, and with puberty comes greater awareness of themselves and their sexuality. However, if you are smart, you will have laid the emotional foundations for this stage long before any physical signs appear.

Pre-pubescent boys often talk about girls and relationships, and 'who loves who' is common playground parlance in junior schools. Your son will almost certainly hear conversations about kissing and dating at the very least, and it is important

> I started dating at fifteen. There was no pressure from
> my peers but I felt a personal pressure. I thought I must
> do it.   *Eighteen-year-old*

from the earliest opportunity to start feeding him information
that is sound, and imbued with the sort of moral spin that you
would like to impart on sex and relationships.

This does not mean that you have to sit him down on
his first day at primary school and give him the time-honoured lecture on 'the birds and the bees'. It is of little use to
have a heart-to-heart when he is too young to understand
what you are saying and, more importantly, not the least
bit interested.

Anyway, you will probably find that an opportunity will
present itself to introduce the topic in the normal course of
events. At around eight or nine years old, your son may make
a comment about a provocative advertisement or something
that happens on TV. It may be that he repeats something he
has heard in the playground. Whatever the occasion, it is a
chance for you to expand the conversation and give him a
fuller understanding of sexual relationships.

What you can do
In the old days, a father was customarily lumbered with the job
of sitting down and explaining the 'facts of life' to his embarrassed son. Most parents now seem to favour the less formal
approach and agree that it can come from either parent or
both, depending on when the opportunity arises. Other tips for
keeping the topic of sexuality as painless as possible for both
you and your son include:

- *Answering questions as honestly as possible.* If you start using quaint euphemisms and analogies, you will end up tied in knots. Better to speak honestly and openly.
- *Acknowledging your embarrassment.* You might as well let on if you find this faintly discomforting because your well-tuned adolescent will be able to tell anyway. It might also help him to reveal that he too is uncomfortable and to relax a little.
- *Not ignoring sexual developments.* If your son has his first wet dream, for example, encourage him to discuss what is happening and how he is feeling. If he cannot talk to you, is there another responsible adult that you trust? Your son needs guidance through these unnerving changes – otherwise, he will garner his knowledge from his friends and it may be a case of the blind leading the blind.
- *Filling out his knowledge.* If you catch your son and his friends repeating rude words or discussing sketchy sexual details, flesh out his knowledge so that he is not floundering under any misconceptions. If the novelty of rude words means he keeps repeating them inappropriately, the general consensus of advice from our panel of parents is to ignore the language but to explain that it can give offence and where and when it is appropriate to use it.

Relationships with girls

It is important to reiterate here that sexuality is an intensely personal and individual thing, and the following description of unfolding events can only be a generalization with the full spectrum of individual permutation in between. So, bear in mind that the timing and nature of relationships are described here in broad brushstrokes.

Until and during early adolescence, children's closest friendships are usually with their own sex, but as they reach the age of about thirteen or fourteen, they may venture into the realm of boy-girl friendships.

As a general rule, they hang out together as a crowd, with the occasional couple pairing off, largely to impress and gain status rather than from any great interest in having a relationship. These pairings are usually brief and superficial with little intimacy, each secretly feeling more comfortable in the company of his or her own sex.

Nonetheless, although not much happens in practice, there is a great deal of talk on the subject of the opposite sex. They compare notes, they speculate on what is happening and, without confessing, they spend a great deal of effort trying to separate the truth from idle boasting.

Unfortunately, boys who brag of numerous sexual experiences are still admired by their friends, and now is the time, if you have not already done so, to start trying to instil the need for sexual responsibility and respect in relationships into your impressionable son. Although some of the chat is harmless, it is worth pointing out that the reputations of girls (and boys) can be compromised by their own lack of judgement or by boastful boys embellishing what has actually taken place.

At fourteen or fifteen, sexual conquests are just status. Like 'I got to third base', but it's no different from when you're older and you have a Mercedes for status. *Twenty-year-old*

Lack of confidence

For boys who have not had much exposure to girls, this is new and unknown territory, and many are simply terrified of looking foolish or getting it wrong. Mothers can teach sons from the earliest age to be relaxed in female company. They can talk to their adolescent sons about what girls like, stressing that conversation, humour and consideration go a long way. This may be a complete revelation to an inexperienced boy. If you can get him comfortable and respectful of girls before he gets into sexual relationships or a heavy romance, you will do him a huge favour.

Many teenage boys actually envy girls – they find them more 'savvy', more poised, more assured. They find it intensely difficult to make conversation so, if your son is shy in female company, encourage opportunities for him to mix with girls, for example at a tennis club or youth group, and help him to foster friendships with the opposite sex.

Early adolescence is a nerve-racking time for boys. They are full of doubts and wonder if any girl will ever like them. Their high sex drive means that they masturbate regularly and they are veterans of sexual pleasure long before they even get a girlfriend. And herein lies the dilemma: at the risk of sounding crude, there is very little that can go wrong with masturbation. However, a sexual relationship with a girl is physically and emotionally fraught with pitfalls. They worry that they may fail in some way and they are emotionally very vulnerable. It is important at this stage to talk openly about sex. Be clear that being in a relationship involves caring, being respectful and careful, and not using others. You can also warn him that girls can be cruel – a mother's insight into the female take on sex and relationships can be both enlightening and an invaluable tool.

As parents, we know that there is much more to sexual encounters than the mere physical experience, but this point can be lost on young lads who only have the benefit of locker-room wisdom to rely on.

Sadly, many boys talk about girls in ugly and disparaging ways. Often, a domineering and disrespectful approach is born from feelings of inferiority or impotence in the face of girls' apparent self-assurance and confidence. Whatever the cause, if young boys hear this attitude and it is not checked or corrected, they may find themselves repeating or adopting it. Ironically, it is older boys and men who have the greatest power to stop this derogatory attitude since if they speak out against it or tell the younger boy to watch his words, it stops.

Dating
These are only ball-park figures, but boys tend to start dating at about fifteen or sixteen while girls are ready to begin a year or so earlier. Parents often take it as an encouraging sign that their children are popular and attractive when they start dating early. However, if your son is not generally very mature, he may struggle to maintain even the most superficial of relationships, and the effort invested can be to the detriment of other interests and activities. So don't be in any rush to get him paired up.

First relationships are usually transient yet adolescents learn a lot about themselves and the opposite sex if they

> There's this battle going on about going out with the lads or staying in with the girlfriends. *Twenty-year-old*

are allowed to move in and out of such associations freely. Nonetheless, some of these early relationships are extremely intense and the misery of breaking up should not be underestimated (see page 72).

In these early liaisons, physical relations are normally limited to heavy petting. However, survey findings suggest that the trend for teenage sexual behaviour in Europe and North America is towards earlier intercourse. According to the National Survey of Sexual Attitudes and Lifestyles 1999–2001, which interviewed 1,000 people, the average age for first sex is now sixteen yet 30 per cent of boys lose their virginity before then. Regrettably, most teenage boys cite peer group pressure and curiosity as their main influences on having sex for the first time. Many are goaded into sexual adventures just to appear one of the crowd and it can be a relief to find out that other boys would also prefer to wait a little (assuming someone is brave or foolhardy enough to confess this).

Despite what you may think, most teenagers are not promiscuous. They actually want what you would like for them – a loving relationship with someone about whom they care deeply. This is particularly true when the teenager is the product of a loving partnership, where this is seen as achievable.

Unfortunately though, a sizeable number of young men still see sex as a challenge – as a mark of adulthood. The fact that a boy can have sex and father a child long

---

Any pressure to have sex is self-induced.

Fifteen-year-old

> In your mid-teens, you just want to find someone to have sex with.
>
> *Seventeen-year-old*

before he is emotionally mature, coupled with the reality that many teenage sexual encounters are opportunistic, means that all too often an unplanned pregnancy is the outcome. This is why it is so important for you to make sure that your son has a good knowledge of contraception long before he needs it (see page 66). You could also give him some insight into the varying shades of attraction, i.e. liking someone, loving someone and lusting after someone. This may give him some sort of understanding of his feelings and help him to realize that he may in fact be 'in love with love', and not the object of his desire (yes, boys can be romantic too).

What you can do

Having spoken to numerous parents representing every view along the moral spectrum about teenage sex, there are a few points worth remembering when it comes to your son's sex life:

- Let him set his own pace.
- Do not put pressure on your son to 'be a man' or to have a sexual relationship simply to become experienced.
- Watch out for the current habit of sexualizing boy-girl relationships at a young age, e.g. asking a seven-year-old 'Who's your girlfriend?'

- Make sure he is well informed on contraception and the facts of life (only 4 per cent of young men in a Tomorrow's Men Survey in 1996 said that they got most of their sex education from their fathers). Your doctor's surgery, local family planning clinic or even the school nurse are all easily accessible places from which to get literature.
- Boys tend to feel distanced by sex education in school and see it as 'girl-orientated'.
- Being given permission to say 'No' is as liberating and empowering for boys as it is for girls.
- If necessary, supply contraception before he is active – it is no good shutting the stable door after the horse has bolted.
- Trust him to be responsible.
- Encourage him to respect women and not to 'use' partners or else he may become a sexual drifter, giving and asking for little.
- Hold onto the thought that boys also want to be loved, not simply to 'have sex'.
- Respect his privacy – sex is intensely personal so do not pry, however tempting.

Teenage pregnancy

As a parent of an adolescent boy, you probably worry yourself sick about him getting beaten up or drink-driving or maybe getting in with 'a bad lot'. Getting a girl pregnant is not necessarily one of the first things to cross your mind when considering dangers. However, without wishing to give you yet one more thing to worry about, the complications of becoming a father in his teens are manifest and manifold.

Contraception

Lack of access to contraception is frequently cited as the reason why no birth control has been used. Therefore, it is down to you as parents to discuss the need for contraception with your son before he is sexually active and, if necessary and if it is not against your moral principles, to supply your son with the necessary literature and/or condoms.

- Get information from your local family planning centre or doctor. Do not rely on your own hazy recollections because methods of contraception change rapidly and you may be out of date.
- Make it clear that a condom is the only way to reduce risk of infection from AIDS (Acquired Immune Deficiency Syndrome).
- Get across the idea that both boys and girls are responsible for contraception.
- Explain how and where to get hold of different devices and how to use the device once they have it.
- Even if your position is against teenage sexual activity, make it clear that if your son encounters trouble of any kind, he can discuss it with you and rely on you for support.

There's a pressure on young women to control their young men – to stop them doing daft things, to stop them putting themselves in dangerous situations. As a bloke, you don't have any understanding of why these pressures are being brought to bear on you. This can lead to the breakdown of perfectly decent relationships.   *Twenty-year-old*

The US and Britain have one of the highest rates of teenage pregnancy in the world – and the fathers are often young men. The effects on teenage mothers have been well documented, but there is very little information on how these events affect adolescent fathers of children born to teenage mothers.

Despite the popular image of the 'callous love rat', it should not be assumed that just because he is young, the teenage father is not interested in the well-being of his child – young fathers are often more interested than the media would have us believe.

A research project in 1997 by Suzanne Speak, *Young Single Fathers: Their involvement in fatherhood*, carried out among young fathers in Newcastle upon Tyne showed that the girl's mother is often the critical factor in whether or not a teenage father has any contact with his child. If the boy enjoys a good relationship with the girl's family (particularly the mother), he is more likely to be included. If, on the other hand, there is a difficult relationship or no relationship, the girl's mother will put pressure on the young mother to sever contact with the father. Given that many teenage mothers are still living in the family home, this pressure can be hard to withstand.

As far as parents of teenage fathers are concerned, it seems they fall into two distinct categories with not much in between. They either wholeheartedly support their son's involvement with the child or they are dead against it. Either way, there is a sense of the parents taking over, and this often pushes the teenage father back into a more dependent role.

Whatever your views on teenage sex and pregnancies, if it happens, it is indisputable that your son will need plenty of emotional (and financial) support, and his first port of call will probably be you.

A young teenage father who stays with the mother and supports the family usually has to give up any thoughts of further education, and he is often limited to the less well-paid jobs. He has less disposable income than his single friends and his freedoms and the spontaneous lifestyle that he previously took for granted are severely curtailed. As he sees his mates going out and having fun, this can lead to resentment and feelings of dissatisfaction with his lot. On top of this, not only is he having to come to terms with the responsibility of fatherhood but this may be his first serious relationship, and he is having to learn how to relate emotionally to his partner. Of course, all this is also true for the young mother, and both will need a great deal of support if they are to successfully negotiate these common problems.

From thirteen to seventeen I wanted one-night stands rather than a relationship. I find the whole idea of commitment a pain in the arse. I feel quite happy as I am.

Nineteen-year-old

■ PROBLEM SOLVING

Sexual abuse

Parents naturally fear the thought of their child being sexually abused. Yet it is not enough to warn your children about strangers, since about 75 per cent of sexual assaults on children are committed by people they know, often family members. Moreover, boys are as vulnerable to abuse as girls.

Children who have been abused often abruptly change their behaviour. They may become withdrawn or depressed, start to do badly at school, drop old friends and/or begin lying, stealing or even run away. Sometimes, they begin to exhibit precocious sexual behaviour, such as trying to arouse an adult, or have an excessive preoccupation with sexual matters. They may develop urinary infections or complain of pain in the genital or anal area as a result of the abuse.

In some cases, it is not a question of sustained abuse but rather a one-off sexual advance from a known adult, such as a sports coach, teacher or club leader, for example. Your son should know that in this situation, he is able to firmly say 'No' to this person, and that he should then tell a trusted adult or yourself without delay.

Sexually transmitted diseases (STDs)
Statistically, adolescents have the highest rate of STDs of any sexually active age group. In part this is due to sexual experimentation coupled with a reluctance to use condoms, and also because the high levels of hormones in the body at puberty make teenagers more susceptible to certain infections.

Some doctors recommend routine tests for STDs for all sexually active adolescents, but this is far from common. If your son suspects he has an STD:

- React calmly and in a matter-of-fact way (you can scream silently in your room later).
- Make sure he goes to the STD clinic for the relevant tests without delay.
- Point out that with the exception of AIDS, all STDs can be treated and cured if detected in time.
- Encourage him to follow the prescribed treatment.
- Despite understandable embarrassment, persuade him to tell anyone he has had sex with, if this is appropriate, so they too can be treated.
- Remember that his sex life is private – encourage him to consult the doctor and to do all of the above, but do not pry for details. Let him know that you will respect the confidentiality between him and his doctor, however hard it may be for you.

If you suspect that your son is being sexually assaulted, introduce the subject of being touched in a general way instead of direct questioning. Children who have been sexually abused are often frightened, ashamed or fearful that it was their fault, and they frequently do not tell their parents. Once you have discussed things in a general way, you can gently encourage him to tell you about anything that has happened specifically to him. Over a period of time, he may feel confident enough to open up to you.

Although it is entirely natural to feel rage, if your child acknowledges being abused it is important that you do not show your anguish to him or he may clam up again. Keep calm and encourage him to describe exactly what has happened, all the time reassuring him that he is not to blame. You must then seek professional help. You could Contact your doctor or the NSPCC's helpline – (tel. 0808 8005000) or Childline (tel.: 0800 1111). Alternatively, contact the local police or Social Services Child Protection team.

Prevention

There are several steps you can take to help protect your children from sexual assault:

- Help your son to differentiate between good and bad touching.
- Teach him how to say 'No'.
- Encourage him to tell rather than keep secrets.
- Reiterate stranger-danger messages.
- Tell him never to accept a lift in a car or go to anyone's house without your knowledge.
- Let him know that he should react to assault by shouting and running away. Molesters do not expect children to be assertive.

Break-up of relationships

The break-up of an early relationship, whether it is heterosexual or homosexual, can be extremely traumatic for an adolescent. It is all wrapped up in fears of inadequacy and rejection, feeling that they can never love anyone as much again, and wondering if there will indeed be anyone again who might be interested in them.

Boys are especially emotionally vulnerable because they lack the empathetic support network that girls rely on. Young men have neither the vocabulary nor the desire to discuss their emotions, and they also consider it weak to show their hurt and frailty. This emotional illiteracy can lead to withdrawal and depression or to expressing their incomprehensible feelings in the only way they know how – anger and violence.

If you have talked to your son about his feelings from the earliest age, he will be better placed to deal with a relationship break-up and all the ensuing emotions of rejection, failure and heartache.

However, if your son is already under stress from exams or pressure of school work, a relationship break-up can be the final straw that pushes him into depression or worse. Consequently, you should be extra vigilant at this time. Encourage

Homosexual relationships

Most teenagers at some time or another have a 'crush' on someone of their own sex. This is particularly common him to speak to you, his closest friends or a trusted adult and do not be fooled by his cavalier attitude and protestations that 'I'm fine. She didn't mean that much to me anyway!' Boys push the hurt inside because they feel that it is manly to be stoical, but they experience emotions just as intensely as girls do, and they too need to talk about it in some way.

What you can do

- Keep a surreptitious eye on your son to make sure that he is not becoming down or depressed.
- Encourage activities with friends that he enjoyed before this relationship.
- Try to prevent your son giving up all other interests, friends and passions when in a relationship. It will be hard because young love tends to be all-consuming.
- Make it clear that you are happy to talk about his break-up at any time and encourage other close friends and relations of your son to do the same.
- If he is severely affected, point out that independent counselling is available.
- If the break-up affects his schoolwork, make the teachers aware.

in single-sex schools or where a teenager does not meet people of the opposite sex very often. Some boys masturbate in each other's company or masturbate each other, but this in itself does not mean that the individual is gay.

Whether your son simply experiences fantasies about his own sex, has a crush on someone he knows or experiments with other boys, for the vast majority this is simply a temporary phase of sexual experimentation. It may be due to a timely combination of high sex drive, curiosity and opportunity, and this passes as heterosexual relationships become more readily and easily accessible.

However, for 10 per cent of boys, homosexual feelings are not just a stage they go through and, for this sizeable minority, this is a confusing and worrying time.

Boys fear homosexuality principally because they do not understand it. All they know for sure (in adolescent wisdom) is that it is not manly or masculine and it invites victimization.

As a result, the fear of homosexual labelling can stop boys from enjoying the physical comfort of touch, not just from their mates but from family too. It sexualizes all touch. What they fail to realize is that homosexual taunts such as 'gay', 'faggot' or 'poof' can be for the most trivial of crimes, such as the wrong hairstyle, clothes or accent – in fact for just about anything. These taunts are especially hurtful because most adolescents are not sufficiently sure of their sexual proclivities to know with certainty that it is not true.

> Girls can be quite aggressive in the way that they deal with blokes. Blokes can be put down in a way that is quite mentally damaging instead of just saying no thanks. *Eighteen-year-old*

What if your son believes he is gay? This is a time when a youngster desperately wants to fit in and to recognize that you are fundamentally different in some way can be quite traumatizing.

Many gay teenagers suppress their feelings or deny them, sometimes for years, which leads to stress and unhappiness. For most, it is the thought of letting their parents down or fear of rejection by their family that keeps them silent. Remember that if your teenage son tells you that he is gay, it is testimony to the strength of your relationship that he feels able to trust you with this news.

For many parents, the disclosure comes as a shock. You may experience real grief for the lost dream of seeing your son having a classic happy family and producing grandchildren. Another common reaction is to be fearful for your child. There are still many prejudiced people who could potentially make your son's life miserable and even put him in physical danger. And more than that, parents fear that their child is moving into a world beyond their reach or understanding. If you hold certain religious beliefs, one of the difficulties you may experience is reconciling these doctrines with your son's gay orientation – you may be ostracized from your church at a time when you need it most for emotional and spiritual support. You may experience an isolating feeling that you are different from other parents and, in this case, it is important to talk to other parents in the same situation. Look out for support groups such as the Family and Friends of Lesbians and Gays (FFALG).

Despite these common reactions, Simon Blake of the National Children's Bureau says, 'A parent's ultimate job is to support and look after your son. Most people come to terms with it but how you react initially can determine how well the family adapts.'

Once the news has sunk in, you might question why your son chose this way of life, but it is not a question of choice. His gay orientation is simply part of him, it is not chosen. Just as you do not choose to be heterosexual, being homosexual is natural for your son.

At this point, many parents ask: 'Where did I go wrong?' This is only an issue if you consider being gay to be a 'problem'. Certainly, the myth that a weak or absent father and a strong, dominant mother can produce a gay son holds no water. If this were the case, during times of war, the women would be raising a generation of homosexual children. And how can you explain families where only one child is gay and yet his siblings, who have been raised in the same way, are not? Unfortunately, parents find it easier to find fault in themselves than to admit the fact that there is a side to their child that they never knew about. This search for a cause inside yourself is a self-inflicted punishment that helps neither you nor your son. In fact, such agonizing is more likely to increase your son's problems.

Another common question for parents of gay teenagers is, 'Will he grow out of it and will he be emotionally scarred if he realizes later on that he's not gay after all?' There is a possibility that your son is bisexual, but the number of practising bisexuals in the population is very small. Given the pressure that a young gay man faces, it is unlikely that your son could believe himself to be gay unless this is his natural sexual proclivity. Rather than clinging on to the hope that he may be going through a phase or is actually bisexual, it is better not to pressure him and to simply give him as much support, love, and understanding as you can muster.

> In GCSE year, one of my friends was rumoured to be gay. He was teased every single day but no one stopped being friends with him. Although it must have been difficult for him, in the end, it was just dropped.
>
> *Eighteen-year-old*

Essentially, you still want the same things you have always wanted for your child. Namely that he lives a happy, well-adjusted, fulfilling life with a loving relationship, and this is still achievable. There are plenty of happy and successful gay men.

What you can do
Remember, your son has trusted you enough to tell you this news, now it is up to you to support him the best way you can. The following pointers can make a difference:

- Be sensitive and loving to ensure that he still feels he can confide in you.
- Try to remember that arguments and threats cannot change your son's sexual orientation but they can damage your relationship irredeemably.
- It is not useful to dwell on 'Where did we go wrong?' The cause of homosexuality is not fully understood, but it is certainly not down to you, so do not beat yourself up.
- Recognize that there is no 'right' or correct way for parents to react in this situation.
- Do not smother your emotions with reason. Some parents say they have come to terms with and accept

their son as he is, even when feeling deeply upset inside. Better to tell him that this is a shock which you are totally unprepared for, that you still love him, but you need time to deal with the shock and to get support, such as that offered by FFLAG.

• Make sure that you and your son have full knowledge of the HIV/AIDS subject and stress that 'safe sex', i.e. using a condom, must be practised. Literature is available from your doctor, STDs or the AIDS charities (see Useful addresses, page 311). Knowledge can dispel risk and fear, so give your son the relevant information.

• Encourage your son to accept himself for what he is and to be happy. Your loving support is the best way for him to achieve this.

■ CASE STUDY – Brenda Oakes' story

Many parents are unprepared for the news that their son is gay. Yet how you react to the news can have important repercussions on your relationship, as one parent found out.

'Michael was eighteen. He was due to go away to university and it would be his first time away from home. He decided a year previously that he should tell us that he was gay. He'd come to the conclusion that he wasn't going to change and that's how he was. Once he'd accepted that he was gay, he wanted to tell us but it took him another twelve months to pluck up the courage.

'He now tells me that he always knew he was different. When he was about eleven or twelve, he began to realize what that difference was. It horrifies me to think of all those years that he went through alone, frightened and worried.

'Before he told us, we didn't have the remotest idea. My husband was a policeman for thirty years and he'd just retired. We had four children (Michael has two older brothers and an older sister) and busy lives. We felt very ignorant.

'I thought Michael had got it wrong. I tried to persuade him that he was wrong because my view of gay people was very negative and I knew my son to be a nice, kind, loving person and I thought, "he can't be right", because the two images were so different.

'I persuaded him to see a counsellor. He went because he is a kind, caring person and he wanted to please me. He only went once and I realized that he did know what he was talking about. Michael was gay.

'I felt very, very shocked. I was worried and anxious – fearful for his future. We wanted to protect him. We wondered what would happen to him. You've got this lovely son who has never been any trouble, a happy little boy that everyone adores as the baby of the family, and suddenly he tells you he belongs to a group of people whom you know nothing about. It was as if he had died. It was a horrible, horrible time. It was like having a stranger in your home that you know nothing about. My husband was very shocked. For him, these were people he had had to arrest as a policeman.

'Initially I blamed everyone – the teachers, the scout master, everyone – my ignorance is laughable now. He just always was and still is gay.

'My husband and I spoke every night into the wee small hours. We realized we knew very little and we had to find out more. I was a mature student at the time, so I found books from the library. We started to talk to people and some months later, we found the Manchester Parents Group and that helped a great deal. It helped to be able to talk freely about something that we felt we had to keep secret at that point.

'For his part, Michael was tremendously relieved once he had told us. We tried to keep our fears from him but I don't think we could. But he was relaxed and very happy. I think he was relieved he had not been thrown out. He said later that he thought we'd be okay, but it still took courage.

'My other children didn't know for two years because Michael was away at university down south. They were busy with their own lives and we didn't know for sure whether Michael wanted them to know. He eventually told his sister and she wanted the boys to know. She was upset and worried. They were shocked and surprised but they were fine. Again they had no suspicion.

'I think Michael worked as hard as he did to get his GCSEs and A levels to get away. It's scary growing up as a little boy surrounded by heterosexuals and feeling different. University probably seemed to him like the best place to be. He was surprised when he came home after a few months to see the change in us. He was impressed that we had made such an effort to understand.

'Finding out that Michael is gay has been life-changing. We didn't know that such a big minority group existed or what a lovely life gay people can have. Just because your son is gay, it doesn't mean he will automatically want to be part of the scene or part of the gay village. He may be very serious-minded and just want to continue with a quiet life.

'We are proud of our gay son and wouldn't change anything about him. We are glad now that we were given an opportunity to learn and grow. We might have remained in ignorance of a large and important minority group in our society, and been so much the poorer for failing to understand what a wealth of human love in its many guises exists on this planet.

'Michael is very happy. Wherever he works, he makes sure he is "out" because he doesn't want to work anywhere where they don't accept him for what he is. Michael is not a campaigner, but he does things in his own quiet way. I'm the one who bangs the drum.

'Parents with gay children start out worried and anxious but, when they get into it, they end up angry at how society treats our kids. That's how I got involved with FFLAG (Families and Friends of Lesbians and Gays). We are just ordinary parents with other kids as well. We just want that one child to be treated the same as our other children and they are not. Our lesbian and gay children are still discriminated against by the law of the land.

'Even now, it's hard to come out. At FFLAG, we've got parents whose son has just told them he's gay and he's thirty-five years old. They can't risk being thrown out of their families. The very nature of parenthood is that the couple are heterosexual so the chance of them really understanding is low.

'The parents who seek out FFLAG* are keen to open their minds – they recognize their own lack of information and want to know more about it. What worries me more are the parents who won't go to a group or admit to themselves that their child is gay. Naturally, there are some people who are not group-oriented, but they can talk to us on the phone. But, if parents go in and shut the door – if they shut their hearts and their minds, they will lose their children. They have to open up.

---

* FFLAG central helpline: 0845 652 0311 or contact info@fflag.org.uk. Check out www.fFlag.org.uk for literature and details on workshops, seminars and training courses

'Some parents get very upset because they realize that their son went through years of being frightened and alone, and yet they couldn't help him because he didn't feel he could tell them that he was gay. That's when it hits them and they get really upset.

'I now say listen to your child, try hard to understand him, and talk to other parents who have been there before you. Remember that it is not that he has changed, but it's that you now know him better.'

5

Rites of passage

Throughout our parenting lives we constantly learn new skills and adjust to new challenges. It seems that no sooner have you got used to dealing with your son at one stage in his development, than he enters another phase of his life and you have to learn how to react and cope all over again.

For example, just as you get comfortable with him being in Key Stage 2 and you start enjoying his new confidence and maturity, he hits the muscle-flexing era of the self-assured nine-year-old and, oh no, here you go again. Should you rein him in or give him his head? Is his backchat playful exuberance or plain rudeness and what do you do for the best?

And, of course, the decisions get more complex and the stakes get higher as your son gets older. Suddenly, you have to be able to make the right judgements about how late your son can stay out alone; whether he is allowed to stay over with 'dubious' friends; if he should be allowed to drink alco-

> Kids use drugs, alcohol and speed to express rebellion or a sense of self-destiny.   *Twenty-year-old*

hol, and if so, how much? Then, just as you are satisfied that you made the right call on the alcohol dilemma, the goalposts move and you need the wisdom of Solomon to decide the right approach to smoking cannabis, for instance.

Try to remember that you do not have to have all the answers on the spot – it is not a quiz show. As he moves from one stage to the next, some decisions are hard to make. You can stall for time. Tell your son that you want to talk it over with your partner or a friend or even to sleep on it before giving a decision. As long as you make sure you always get back to him with an answer, giving yourself a little breathing space to make a decision without pressure is okay.

As usual, there are certain ages and developmental and educational milestones that portent changes in your son's behaviour and, if you know when these stages roughly occur, you are better equipped to deal with the ensuing changes in behaviour.

Puberty is an obvious milestone that brings with it very blatant changes. However, there are other, less overt, land-marks in your son's life, which can also herald new begin-nings. These may be considered of great significance by your son or the effects may simply be noticed by you. The following are some of the most common rites of passage experienced by parents and sons the world over.

Top dog syndrome
By the time your son has reached the last two years at pri-mary school, he is likely to feel pretty confident in his school environment. Self-esteem should be high and he and his fel-low classmates consider themselves pretty big fish in a small pond.

He has also formed good friendships by now. Whereas 'best friends' changed by the day at ages seven or eight, by ten and eleven, his friends are an important and fairly fixed part of his life – they are people who share his interests and values, who support and help him, and whom he wants to emulate and impress.

This self-assurance in his own environment coupled with the need to score brownie points with his friends, may mean that your son develops a cocky bravado, which is at its worst when his friends are around. He may give you cheek, answer back and generally act 'big' when his friends are present, even if he is relatively polite at home normally.

Most parents have a natural reluctance to humiliate their sons in front of their friends and, for this reason, some put off correcting backchat until they are alone with the perpetrator. Other parents find this uncharacteristic rudeness intolerable and react immediately with a private or a public reprimand. Whatever your inclination, rudeness should not go unchecked. As we saw before, it is not that you have to pull your son down a peg or two, far from it, but he needs to realize that he should respect others and that rudeness is unacceptable in your home. It is also worth pointing out to him that his friends are not impressed but they are embarrassed when they see him being rude to his parents – a point that often passes young adolescents by.

For what it is worth, his new-found cockiness is about to be shaken as he passes into his new school, and his status as top dog is reversed. However, if this does not curb his bluster, hold on to the thought that most boys develop some humility and are less self-absorbed at about the age of fifteen.

New school

By the time they come to change schools at eleven, many boys are excited about moving on. They feel they have outgrown their primary schools and are looking forward to the broader horizons of secondary education. They definitely view a new school as a rite of passage – a move into a more adult world.

Secondary school is generally very different from primary education. Your son will have to fit in to a more complex social system with fuller academic and extra curricular opportunities and choices. He will be in a class that is drawn from a wider geographic area and very probably a wider social mix.

Most adolescents thrive in this new environment, while a few resist it and others are simply overwhelmed by the enormity of the change. The major obstacles reported by Year 7 children are:

- Adjusting to being the youngest and littlest after being the eldest and biggest.
- Getting used to increased amounts of homework – it can be hard to fit everything in.
- Finding your way around – secondary schools are usually considerably larger than primary schools, and getting lost during the first few weeks can be upsetting.
- New teachers – with a new teacher for each subject, there are many new and important adults to adjust to.
- The transition is exhausting – many parents remark on how tired the new Year 7 pupils are, particularly during the first few terms. They appear to be physically and emotionally exhausted from moving about

the school, from the increase in sport in the curriculum, and from getting used to the new timetable. This is in addition to an earlier start to the day and possibly a longer journey.

• So much to remember – many children find that remembering homework, books, and the right kit on the right day is a strain.

Moving to a new school is such a major rite of passage in a child's life and most parents are vigilant and sensitive to how it may affect their child. If you can take an interest in your son's new life, encourage him in his pursuit of new interests, pastimes and friendships, and support him in his choices, he should thrive.

However, not all parents cope with this milestone as well as their children. For those of you who were very involved in your son's primary school activities, you may feel excluded by a secondary school approach which does not encourage parents to be so hands on. You may know less about your son's daily life than ever before and, for some parents, cutting the apron strings can be very hard.

If you find yourself feeling this way, do the best you can to take a step back. Admittedly, it is hard to cut loose your cherished child to make his own mistakes. Although he must make his own choices, if you have always talked, there is every hope that you will be consulted in the decision-making process. You are not losing your son to a school system and friends you do not even know – you are accompanying him on an exciting and thrilling adventure. If you show an interest, he will happily include you, but do not crowd him or try to take control.

Pornography

Picture this, if you will. You walk into your fourteen-year-old's bedroom to collect the dirty washing strewn over the floor and, while searching for a rogue sock, you discover his horde of pornographic magazines under his bed. Do you:

a) Fly into a rage and berate your son for being a 'dirty little bugger'?
b) Pretend not to have noticed, slip from the room and immediately call your best friend for a reassuring chat?
c) Flick through the mag regretting that you no longer look that good in a G-string?

Sadly, the knee-jerk reaction of answer (a) is probably the most common response to this time-honoured scenario. Many parents go off the deep end about pornography, which frequently has the adverse effect of pushing your son into a greater interest in the subject or drives him underground, making his viewing somehow more furtive and seedy.

Yet why are you surprised that your son has pornography? Did you think he would be more enlightened than most? Let's be realistic. Boys like to look at naked women. Thankfully, it is normally a passing interest on his way to discovering his own sexuality, and before entering into a relationship. There are even those that argue that pornography can be informative.

In some cases, it can be mildly amusing. A neighbour was delighted to see her eight-year-old engrossed for hours making a wonderful collage from magazine clippings. He proudly showed her the finished artwork and, on closer inspection, she realized that the montage was made up entirely from the women's underwear section of her home shopping catalogues. She did not know whether to laugh or cry, but she certainly did not want this particular work of art pinned on the fridge door!

Irrespective of your views on pornography, and most of us have strong feelings on this subject, your son's motives are fuelled by a natural curiosity and this, in itself, is not unhealthy. Whether you accept it or ban it, he should not be shamed for being interested.

In reality, the biggest dilemma for most parents arises when your son wants to put pictures of naked women on his bedroom walls. Do you allow him to do so because it is his bedroom or do you not permit this in your house?

I have to say the jury was split on this one when we asked our panels of parents and experts. Surprisingly, opinion was completely polarized. However, everyone did agree that it is important to discuss the issue with your son. Ask him why he wants the pictures on his wall? Is he aware of how this makes his mum/sister feel?

This can lead to a more general discussion about the purpose and effects of pornography, i.e. does it degrade women? Is it exploitative? In this way, you can provoke him into deeper thought about the issue, and together you can come up with a family approach to the use of pornography.

As a word of warning, you should make sure that you and your partner are clear on your united parental attitude to pornography before you speak to your son. There is no point in one of you being very sensible and politically correct if the other one is furtively nudge, nudge, wink, winking with him. If the male partner's excuse is that it did not do him any harm when he was a lad, it should be pointed out that pornography is much more explicit now than it was in his day, and that Internet hardcore pornography is easily accessible to any young adolescent with a computer.

What you can do

Whatever your stance on pornography, it is worth remembering that these are not impossible waters to navigate (if you keep a sense of humour), and that the issues are not black and white. General facts and tips for handling the subject sensitively include:

- Encourage your son to think about the messages the pictures send.
- If you are not going to prohibit pornography, you could help him to find more suitable erotica.
- Make sure that the material that boys pass around is not objectionable and that Internet access is controlled.
- Age makes a difference – what may be tolerated in a fourteen-year-old is not necessarily suitable for under-thirteens, where erotica may prematurely sexualize boys.
- Be aware that for the shy or gauche teenager, masturbating while looking at pornography is easier than embarking on a relationship with a real girl.
- Pornography can have an added allure for boys who are not used to seeing nudity or who grow up in a predominantly male household.
- Too much exposure to pornography can depersonalize women and sex, and it can become addictive.

Alcohol

Booze is a problem for teenage boys. About 60 per cent of under-age children (thirteen- to seventeen-year-olds) have bought and tried alcohol, and one-third of this age group drink something at least once a week. In 2000, the mean alcohol consumption for boys who had drunk in the last week was 11.7 units – that is an awful lot of beer.

Although alcohol can have devastating effects, the problem is that it is freely available, socially acceptable and affordable. Young people equate it with being grown up and if they see their parents drinking routinely, they are less likely to meet with objections.

Once again, it is boys who are more likely to experiment with alcohol than girls, and they are also more likely to become dependent upon it. It is the drug of choice for many sporting young men who use it as a bonding experience after the match.

Unfortunately, however, teenage boys seem incapable of using alcohol in moderation as a social device for these bonding experiences. More often, they drink to excess with 37 per cent of young men aged sixteen to twenty-four regularly drinking twice the recommended daily limits of alcohol and 60 per cent of fifteen-year-olds saying that they have been drunk at least twice.

A boy in our class does not drink and everyone calls him gay. At fifteen, if you can drink eight pints in an evening, you are a god. *Sixteen-year-old*

> Being able to hold your drink is equated with manliness. *Eighteen-year-old*

Being drunk is a rite of passage for adolescent males. To be able to 'hold your drink' is a matter of male pride. In traditional societies, a rite of passage was an opportunity for a boy to prove his courage. Today, high risk drinking is one of the only ways a boy can gain acceptance and join other boys in a test of 'courage' and endurance.

For boys, being willing to take a risk is synonymous with being a man, and excessive alcohol is the natural progression in risk taking. An incidental but important by-product of heavy drinking is that the boy feels invincible and beyond danger when drunk.

Boys use alcohol as the basis for a good time and as a way to break down emotional barriers. We all know men who become maudlin after a few drinks, but these expressions of emotion are forgiven because it happens while drinking which is a manly pursuit. In fact, just about any action is excused the next day on the pretence that a boy was drunk. What a gift for an insecure, self-conscious teenager.

Drinking allows boys to be more emotionally expressive and socially at ease. For the gauche adolescent, alcohol temporarily dulls anxiety, inhibition and loneliness. In addition, getting drunk makes them appear more manly in

> Fourteen to fifteen is the serious drinking period and it dies off by sixteen. *Twenty-year-old*

> The attitude of your parents strongly affects when you
> start drinking.   *Fifteen-year-old*

the eyes of their contemporaries and grants them acceptance into the group. You have to admit, it is an attractive
proposition.

What you can do
The only piece of good news about under-age drinking is that
within a family where occasional social drinking is accepted
as a pleasant part of normal life, most teenagers eventually
learn how to drink sensibly and safely. You can help them to
achieve this goal:

- ***Do not impose an outright ban.*** Firstly, it would be
  hypocritical if you like the odd tipple yourself and adolescents resent anything that smacks of inconsistency
  or double standards. Secondly, prohibition is more
  likely to provoke your youngster into drinking more, in
  the true spirit of teenage rebellion.
- ***Try to instil the principle of moderation.*** If you can
  help him to recognize when he has had enough, you will
  be doing your son a great favour. Make it clear to him
  that it takes more courage to say 'no more' in the face of
  peer pressure, than to cave in and have another drink.
- ***Teach him the tricks of the trade.*** Strategies for
  keeping his alcohol intake unobtrusively low will stand
  him in good stead, i.e. keeping half a glass in front of
  him so that it is not continuously replenished; sticking
  in a smaller round with the slower drinkers; asking for

water or a soft drink every other round due to 'a terrible thirst'; surreptitiously buying himself a low-alcohol lager when it is his turn at the bar, and so on.

- **Line his stomach before going out for the night.** It may seem like an old wives' tale, but drinking a glass of milk or having a heavy meal before going out on the town can delay the rate at which alcohol is absorbed from the stomach.

- **Prohibit driving after drinking.** Make sure that he fully grasps the importance of this and that he never allows himself to be driven by anyone who has been drinking.

- **Monitor his drinking.** Turning a blind eye to bouts of binge drinking is not the answer. If he sees you drinking in moderation and you give him guidance on his own intake, he is more likely to cope well with teenage drinking.

Smoking

Health education programmes that target young people have been spectacularly unsuccessful in campaigning against smoking. In fact, there has been an increase in young smokers, particularly young women.

Many children try their first cigarettes by smoking the stubs from their parents' ashtrays. Others are introduced to the habit by friends when they start socializing independently of you. However, if your son has not started smoking by the time he is twenty, there is a good chance that he will never become a smoker.

> I know smoking is bad for me, but if I want to risk it, that's my business. *Seventeen-year-old*

Unfortunately, the well-documented health risks of smoking will probably not influence your teenage son very much. Teenagers invariably believe that they are invincible and effects that may or may not be experienced in thirty or forty years' time are of little interest to them now. However, new research published in 2002 from Sapporo in Japan using an advanced new scanning technique, shows that smokers aged between eighteen and thirty-five display signs of damage associated with coronary heart disease even though they appear healthy on standard cardiac diagnostic tests. It seems that the harmful effects of smoking begin to significantly accumulate much earlier than was previously thought.

If statistics do not cut any ice with your smoking teenage son, try the following:

- Being young does not counteract the harmful effects of smoking.
- If he is sporty, take the approach that smoking reduces stamina, decreases muscle tone, and slows reflexes.
- Point out that having smoky hair, clothes and breath are not attractive.
- Avoid preaching – this could drive your son from a mild inclination to smoke into a fierce determination to do so just to spite you.
- Be cautious about banning cigarettes – you do not want your son secretly smoking in his room and setting fire to bedding etc.
- If he develops a habit and is having difficulty giving up, encourage him to follow a programme, and to accept outside help.

> People make informed decisions about drugs. It's not
> a reckless action.   *Seventeen-year-old*

Drugs

Most teenage boys like to experiment and your son will almost
certainly have been offered drugs at some time during his
secondary education. For those who do take drugs, most
use 'soft' drugs, and usually at a party with friends. This is
because, like alcohol, it makes them feel less inhibited and
gives them a 'buzz'.

To parents, the reason why your son might try drugs when
the risks are so obvious is unfathomable. But young men do
not think like adults and, for them, the reasons can range from
being goaded into it by macho friends to being a thrill-seeker
who likes to test his own limits. This particular rite of passage
involves doing something that is breaking the law – a very
grown-up occupation – which certainly adds spice for the
young lad trying to prove his valour.

The fact is that drug taking among the young is on the
increase – drug use among fourteen- to fifteen-year-olds
has increased eight-fold since 1987 and the UK has more
fifteen-to sixteen-year-old drug users than any other EU
country. In 2000, 14 per cent of children aged eleven to
fifteen had used drugs in the last year compared to 11 per
cent in 1998, with cannabis being the most likely drug to
be used.

Yet, of those adolescents who experiment with drugs
(again boys are more likely to do so), only a small minority
progress from 'soft drugs' to 'hard' drugs such as heroin, or to
dependency. As a broad generalization, those who become

> If people want stuff they can get anything you like in
> twenty- four to forty-eight hours.   *Sixteen-year-old*

drug- or alcohol-dependent, tend to take these substances as
a way of solving or escaping personal problems.

What you can do
Burying your head in the sand and hoping that your son is
not exposed to drugs is foolhardy in the extreme. In today's
society, he will in all probability come across drugs at some
time. You can play an important part in preparing him for
how he deals with the situation, and in minimizing the risks:

- *Stay well informed.* There is plenty of literature out
  there, so make sure that you are up to speed on drugs
  and their effects, and then discuss the issues with your
  son. Give him the information to digest. If he understands the risks involved, he stands a better chance of
  making an informed decision if drugs are offered.
- *Stay calm and keep things in perspective.* If you
  catch your son having a crafty puff at a joint, do not
  overreact. By all means, make your position on drugs
  clear but do not condemn him as a future addict on
  this evidence alone. Soft drugs are now part of mainstream society – you may find that his friends' parents
  use recreational drugs, or you may partake yourself.
- *Be realistic.* Using scare-mongering techniques,
  such as saying that all drugs are equally harmful, will
  not wash. Make it clear which drugs are potentially the
  most damaging.

> There's plenty of information about drugs. The advice
> is not 'don't do it' but 'do it safely'. People think about
> it and weigh the risks.   *Fifteen-year-old*

- *Build his confidence.* If your son has good self-
  esteem and confidence, he is better placed to resist
  pressure from friends.
- *Express your concerns.* Let him know that it is
  the risks to his mental and physical health, the fact
  that he could be expelled from school, and the legal
  aspects that motivate your concern rather than any
  desire to take the moral high-ground or to be controlling. Parents say that teenagers respond better to this
  approach.
- *Be practical.* It is worth pointing out that if he gets a
  criminal record through possession or supply of drugs,
  certain careers will be barred to him. In England and
  Wales, just over 9,500 children aged ten to seventeen
  were found guilty of or cautioned for drug offences in
  1999, four times the number in 1992 and over thirty
  times the number in 1981.
- *Be aware.* Drug culture varies from area to area
  and school to school, depending on what is fash-
  ionable and affordable. Find out by chatting to your
  son and his friends about what is happening in
  your area and in his social group. You could also
  speak to local police and health specialists for a
  broader picture.
- *Prohibit driving after drug taking.* Just as important as condemning drink-driving, make sure that if

he takes drugs, he fully grasps the importance of not driving afterwards, and that he never allows himself to be driven by anyone who has been partaking. Traffic accidents while under the influence of drugs are on a steady increase and it is a problem that needs to be addressed.

- ***Watch for telltale signs.*** If you suspect that drug use is becoming a regular or daily part of your son's life, it is time to seek help. Telltale signs of drug abuse include:
  - Loss of appetite.
  - Bloodshot eyes, dilated pupils, a runny nose, hacking cough or more colds and infections than usual.
  - General lethargy.
  - Mood changes.
  - Uncharacteristic irritability or aggression.
  - Secrecy.
  - Altered sleeping patterns.
  - Dropping off in schoolwork.
  - Change of friends.
  - Much less or much more cash than usual may indicate that he is buying or selling drugs.
  - The disappearance of cash or valuables.

■ PROBLEM SOLVING

My son is a drug addict

You may recognize that your drug-dependent son has a problem, but until he acknowledges this and actually wants to give up, there is little that can be done to help.

In the past, parents were advised to cut off funds so that the addict was eventually forced, through desperation, to seek help. More recently, it is recommended that parents continue to give their adolescent money, so that he will not be forced to steal to feed his habit. This effectively keeps lines of communication open, despite a possible withdrawal from family life, and when he eventually seeks help, you can be there to offer support.

What you can do
Once he has made a commitment to give up, there is a great deal that you can do:

- *Persuade him to get professional help without delay.* Some hospitals have addiction units or there are very effective self-help groups tailored to different types of abuse. Your doctor should be able to put you in touch with the relevant people or call the National Drugs Helpline (freephone 0800 776600).
- *If he is injecting heroin.* Treat it as a medical emergency and see your doctor straight away. Withdrawal from heroin must be done under supervision and in a hospital to control painful withdrawal symptoms.
- *Offer practical support.* It is difficult to remain drug-free, so help him to stay away from his previous environment and friends, and help him to start a new life.
- *Help him to fill his time.* A job or fulfilling full-time education can give him a new purpose and help him to avoid having too much time on his hands.
- *Will he see a therapist?* Often there is a root cause for drug abuse and a therapist may help your son resolve the problems that made him turn to drugs in the first place.

- **Do not despair if he goes back on drugs.** Although it is hard to stay optimistic, it is very common for addicts to return to drugs on more than one occasion. Hopefully, the drug-free intervals will get longer each time until he is eventually free of the habit.

Losing his virginity

If you ask an adult when he felt he became a man, his reflex response will probably be 'When I lost my virginity.'

Give him time to consider and he may revise his answer, but that is not the point. The point is that losing his virginity is very important to an adolescent boy, something tangible that he equates to becoming a man, and its significance stays with him for a long time.

As we saw in Chapter Four, first sexual encounters are happening earlier and a boy may feel enormous pressure from his peer group and society in general to 'prove his manhood'. He may believe that this is some kind of mystical rite of passage and that once he has 'lost his virginity', he will automatically be bestowed with manly qualities and feelings.

However, because the motives for 'having sex' are often external, he can feel let down or disappointed by the experience. He may even be humiliated by the encounter if he thinks he did it wrong in some way. Teenage girls can be very cruel on occasions and they tend to be more emotionally mature, and better able to handle early sexual encounters.

Manly stoicism will probably prevent your son from discussing his feelings, but if you notice behaviour in him that belies his apparent pride in his new-found sexual conquest, it may be worth giving him openings to discuss his feelings.

For many men, the courage or opportunity to express their disappointment in this 'false summit' does not come until years later. Nonetheless, if you are mindful of the advice given in Chapter Four on sexuality and sexual encounters, then you are well placed to spot any signs of disillusionment or to help prepare your son to deal sensitively with this obviously significant rite of passage.

Depending on the sort of relationship they enjoy, dads can be a good source of reassurance on this particularly sensitive issue. Not so much a heart-to-heart, but more an empathetic 'my first time was disastrous' approach can be very heartening to a young man suffering from dented pride and lack of confidence.

Leaving school

Both parents and children alike recognize leaving school as a major step in moving from childhood to adult life. Whether they are leaving to enter further education or a job, it is a momentous occasion.

Although most young people are relieved that exams are over and welcome the new challenge, most have some regrets at leaving familiar environments and old friends. Boys, in particular, seem unnerved by the change. In the *Leading Lads* survey, life satisfaction scores dropped dramatically when they experienced a move from school to college or work, particularly at ages seventeen and nineteen respectively. In fact, by eighteen to nineteen, over one-quarter of young men had low self-esteem compared with only 6 per cent at age thirteen.

Parents too may experience some trepidation on behalf of their young sons, knowing that college or work may not be easy, and worrying about how he might cope independently. It is usually a time of mixed feelings – relief and pride that your son has reached near-adulthood unscathed and with family relations intact, yet trepidation as you become less actively involved in protecting him from the outside world. There may also be concerns about career or university choices and whether there will be a job at the end of it. Nevertheless, on balance, it should be a time for celebration and looking forward as your son enters a new phase in his life.

Driving

Road accidents are probably a parent's greatest fear when they have teenage sons and rightly so. Statistically, teenage boys are nearly four times more likely to die in a traffic accident than girls, and the figure for road deaths is frighteningly high. In Britain in 2001, 3,443 people were killed and 37,094 were seriously injured on our roads.

Basically, young men can be reckless drivers. Boys aged seventeen to nineteen are the most likely to have an accident, hence the heavy insurance premiums, and young men on motorbikes are even more of a liability.

As soon as he is old enough, your son will want a car. Passing his driving test is a tangible rite of passage and it opens up never before dreamt of freedoms. Never mind that it brings with it great danger – a young lad does not give that a second thought.

> I've been driving six months and I've had a speeding ticket. *Eighteen-year-old*

Of course, you can try to stop him having a car or motor-bike, but if he is stumping up the cash himself from a part-time job, there is little you can do to prevent it.

What you can do
However, if you have a teenage son on the road, there are certain precautions you can take to protect him:

- ***Make sure he gets proper driving lessons.*** He needs professional tuition and, although you can give him the extra practice he needs, he should be taught the rudiments by a trained expert.
- ***Give them extra tuition.*** Driving lessons will get him through his test but it will not give him any experience of driving on a motorway or on windy country roads. Some driving schools provide extra instruction in these specific road conditions but if not, make sure you give him some practice before letting him loose alone.
- ***Make sure the vehicle is structurally and mechanically safe.*** Perversely, many parents buy an old banger for their inexperienced teenage son, while they ride around in a car equipped with all the latest safety technology. If finances permit, get him a modern car with multiple safety features. Whatever you buy, choose something mechanically reliable (you do not want him hitching home in the middle of the night because he has broken down) and slow. Despite what they say about being careful and having fast reactions, young men cannot handle high speed safely.

  A friend presented his teenage son with an old Land-rover on his eighteenth birthday. The reasoning:

it carries plenty of people, it is reliable, it has got a top speed flat out of about 65 mph (105 km/hour) if your ears can stand the rattling racket, and if he hits something, it is built like a tank. Sounds reasonable.

- *Try to talk him out of a motorbike.* All kids are keen to get a set of wheels as soon as possible, but try to persuade him to wait until he can have a car. Use statistics and bribery if necessary. If your plan fails and he is still hell-bent on a motorbike or moped, make sure that he follows a reputable training scheme and provide him with good protective clothing and the best helmet you can afford.

  Most accidents occur in the first six months of riding, so at least try to persuade him to wait until the better weather to start riding a motorbike.

- *Stress the importance of not driving after drinking.* Driving while under the influence of drink is one of the commonest causes of road accidents, and teenagers are among those most likely to die or be severely injured as a result. Therefore, you must be firm on this one, even if it means your son leaves his car at home and you have to collect him (and probably his mates) late at night. This is better than having the temptation of drink-driving. Do not forget to stress that he should never travel as a passenger in cars driven by friends who have been drinking either.

Gap-year travel

Each year more than 200,000 British backpackers set off, 50,000 of whom are teenagers. A gap year before or after university is becoming increasingly popular and, according to one survey, only 17 per cent of parents try to dissuade their teenagers from going, despite the obvious fears for their safety.

For the adventurous teenage boy, gap-year travel is the chance to experiment, to test himself, and to find his limits. It is a great opportunity, and probably his first, to make all key decisions for himself and to rise or fall by them. A heady inducement to any young man.

Yet, for the parents, the overwhelming emotion is one of impotence. You can keep in touch by email, skype and the occasional phone call but, in reality, you will go weeks if not months without hearing, and often you are only contacted when top-up funds or help is required.

You should not take this as a slight on your parent–child relationship, nor as a rejection. The simple reality is that your son is having a whale of a time and he is completely engrossed in his new and absorbing experience.

Meanwhile, you are checking your e-mail in-box every few hours and waiting expectantly for news. Few parents begrudge their children this wonderful opportunity to broaden their horizons, to have fun, and to learn to stand on their own two feet. Nonetheless, this may be tinged with fear for their safety and irritation at not knowing what is going on. Even if your son is thoughtful enough to give you an itinerary, there are no guarantees that it will not alter on a whim – and you will probably be the last to know.

On his return, you will be regaled with tales of daring-do and near-misses, and it is wonderful to see adventure through the eyes of the young. In the meantime, what should you do to make the waiting bearable?

What you can do

These suggestions come from parents whose sons have had a gap year:

- *Keep your fears for his safety in perspective.* Of the many thousands who travel safely each year, only twelve British back-packers were murdered between 1994 and 2000. And to give you greater peace of mind, make sure that he has a copy of the Suzy Lamplugh Trust's *Your Passport to Safer Travel* published by Thomas Cook Publishing (2001) in his luggage.
- *Talk to other parents.* Swapping gap-year horror stories with other parents is strangely therapeutic. Most are trivial and simply serve to remind you that the travellers are still children in many ways, but it helps to know that you are not alone.
- *Keep in touch.* Even if a response to your e-mails or receiving a phone call is rare, it is a reassuring safety net for your son to get news from home, so keep sending letters to the poste-restante.
- *Expect the unexpected.* A phone call from San Francisco asking for details of your son's flight arrival times when you thought he was grape picking in the South of France; receiving photos of him paragliding in the Himalayas when he has always protested a fear of heights; greeting a Venezuelan teenager who does not speak English on your doorstep because your son gave her your address with the 'If ever you're in England' quip. These are just some of the surprises that other parents have experienced. Who knows what you might get …

- ***Stay calm.*** If you get a panicky phone call in the small hours of the morning, keep a level head, and give sound, practical advice. If he senses your fear, he will panic even more. You are a long way from offering immediate practical help, so think strategically. Most situations resolve themselves satisfactorily and sometimes a simple answer is blindingly obvious to you, but it has escaped your intelligent but fallible teenage son.

■ CASE STUDY – Erica's story

Problems at school can have far-reaching repercussions, as one mother finds out.

'I'm sitting at my desk putting the final touches to an article. Tonight, I have to host a major music festival for a charity, giving a talk and acting as MC, with an audience of 800 people.

'At 4 p.m., as I'm about to think of the work for the evening, my sixteen-year-old's headmaster calls me. "Are you sitting down?" he asks. "What's happened?" I reply. "Jeremy has been found with drugs at school."

'It was such a shock. I went straight in to see the headmaster and then somehow struggled through the concert in a daze.

'When we spoke to Jeremy, he explained that they were going to a party on Saturday and someone at school had asked him if he could get some dope. He got it from someone on the bus and foolishly took it into school to give to his friends.

'He was completely pulled up short by the potential of getting a police record. It was also a matter of weeks before his GCSEs and the thought of not doing them was really terrible after he'd worked so hard. He had to look very starkly at the possible consequences of what he'd done.

'In light of the fact that it was a first offence and Jeremy had an unblemished school record, the headmaster allowed him to return to school. I know it sounds mean, but I found out this news on the Friday but I let Jeremy sweat over the week-end to teach him a lesson.

'After the initial emergency response, there are lots of other little considerations that have to be thought about. Like, I had to keep it secret from his grandparents who simply wouldn't understand. I also wanted him to be separated from the boys in question when he returned to school.

'The biggest surprise was the reaction from other parents, some of whom were friends, who were baying for blood and wanted Jeremy excluded. Their holier than thou attitude was sickening because it could have been any one of their sons.

'I'd not given it much thought before, but now I'm amazed at Jeremy's innocence and stupidity at taking dope into school. But also, I realize the hypocrisy of being outraged about him having dope. They've all tried it, I now find out, and we don't even bat an eyelid when our kids get drunk on alcohol.

'Jeremy was very lucky. His headmaster offered him and our family support at a difficult time and was very understanding. If he had been less enlightened or the other parents had had their way, it could have been a very different story.'

6

Communication

As Chapter One demonstrated, boys are prone to bottling up their emotions. They are not keen to talk about their feelings because they view this as a sign of weakness and, rightly or wrongly, they believe that they lack a support network when they are feeling low.

If, on top of a natural male reticence, you add the tendency for all teenagers to become even less communicative, especially during adolescence, then it is little wonder that depression and suicide is so prevalent amongst young men.

Keeping channels of communication open with your son can prove a real challenge, particularly if you are met with monosyllabic answers or a shrug but, without wishing to sound glib, you should never give up. It is essential to establish good reasonable communication with your son from the outset, to be in the best position to ride the 'non-communicative' adolescent years.

However, do not get too comfortable on the moral high ground of 'I've tried but he just doesn't respond'. One of the biggest gripes that young men have about their families,

> Parents are trying to be helpful but it's almost like they're sticking their nose in.   *Sixteen-year-old*

according to the *Leading Lads* survey, is that they 'don't listen to my problems and views'. Boys feel that their parents are controlling and 'seldom talk about things that concern me'.

There you have it. Parents find boys uncommunicative and boys think their parents do not listen to them. A perfect example of a breakdown in communications, wouldn't you say? So, what can you do about it? If you wait for your son to make the first move, it is probably not going to happen.

Firstly, boys need to be furnished with the skills to recognize and express their feelings (see Chapter Seven), and to ask for and receive the support and help they so obviously crave. Secondly, you need to persevere. If you are able to talk and listen to your son and vice versa, your relationship can be based on mutual understanding, consideration and respect. You just never know when your normally tight-lipped son might strike up a dialogue of real depth and importance – it happens, and often at the most unlikely times. A grounding of good communication can help to avoid potential problems and to sort out those that will inevitably arise at some point.

Here are some techniques adapted from professionals and others supplied by parents that may help to promote better communication and understanding between you and your son.

Getting him to talk

Anyone who has ached for their child to tell them what is troubling him will tell you that getting him to open up is easier said than done. Busy lives mean that you can easily fall into the routine of asking about what kind of day your son has had, getting a one-line answer and then going your separate ways.

In fact, research presented to the British Psychology Society in 1997 by Professor Philip Zimbardo, an American psychologist at Stanford University, showed that on average, working parents spend only eight minutes per day talking to their children, and then it is largely to give instructions. If you do not chat together routinely, what hope do you stand of getting your son to open up when there is a burning issue that you feel needs discussion?

It is worth getting into the habit of making time to talk and to be emotionally available to your son. This means giving your full attention to the conversation – not an easy task for time-pressed parents. Do not try to talk while still ironing or with the potato peeler fidgeting in your hand – think how you would feel if you only got half your partner's attention when you wanted to discuss something important. Being distracted is not the same as sideways talking, where you are both involved in an activity. If you concentrate on what he is telling you, you will be surprised by what you can learn when you least expect it.

Gain his trust and get him used to talking to you by chatting about things that interest him. Even if the Premier League, for instance, leaves you cold, at least you are opening up communication channels and it is nice for him to be able to talk to you about something of which he has superior knowledge. What about the music he likes? Make it a conversation rather than an inquisition and you may be surprised at how he gushes.

To initiate a conversation with your son, you are bound to rely on questioning him about his daily life. If you want the conversation to last longer than a nanosecond, get into the habit of using open questions and statements. These involve questions that require something other than a simple 'Yes', 'No' or 'Huuh' answer. For example:

Parent: Did you have a good time at Cubs?
Son: Yep.

Could be replaced by:

Parent: Anything interesting happen at Cubs tonight?
Son: Blah, blah, blah ...

As you can see, you will get a longer reply if the question is open. Similarly, you can tease a conversation from your son by using incomplete phrases that beg an ending:

Mum: So, you were saying that you and James had a bit of a
falling-out today ...

A pregnant pause should encourage him to fill the gap and continue talking.

Adolescents who may be reluctant to talk about their personal life, love to talk about issues that affect them and their friends, such as drugs and under-age drinking. They are also passionate about social issues and global problems, such as the environment or the possibility of nuclear war. Why not their views for once? Allow him to sound off without giving the impression that you have heard it all before or that his ideas are at best idealistic, at worst insane. You do not have to agree, but if you show that you are listening, that you respect his opinions and find them interesting, he is more likely to approach you when he needs to discuss issues closer to home.

When talking in general, make sure you sometimes talk about feelings, not just facts. This does not necessarily come naturally to boys, but if you reveal something of your real self to them (not just the capable, omnipresent, 'I know best' parent), they are more inclined to trust you and in return let you see who they are.

Although it is useful to build some peaceful time into your schedule for your son – perhaps when younger children have gone to bed or when you say goodnight to him – do not expect him to always fit in with your timetable. You are more likely to find that he wants to talk at the least convenient time possible. Wherever possible, seize the moment and give him your full attention because you may not get a second chance. If it really is an impossible time, explain to him why and agree a time when you can talk as soon as possible – and make sure that you stick to it.

Boy's talk

Whereas most women like nothing better than a heart-to-heart, sitting down and intensely looking into your son's eyes and asking him how he feels is anathema to most boys. It makes them extremely uncomfortable and is virtually guaranteed to make him clam up.

Boys prefer to talk in generalities rather than about themselves, and 'sideways-on', while involved in a joint activity, rather than face to face. Armed with this knowledge, if you suspect something is troubling your son, try to do an activity together before you instigate the conversation. It does not much matter what it is: walking, cooking, playing football, anything enjoyable that lessens the intensity of the situation, and that allows you to introduce the topic in a casual fashion. You may even find that your son raises the subject if he feels sufficiently relaxed. In my experience, car rides with just the two of you or, when he is younger, sitting reading a book together are good ways to cut down the tension of an important conversation. In both cases you are naturally side by side rather than head on.

And once he gets going, resist the temptation to interrupt. However well-intentioned, your urge to give advice, finish his faltering sentence or to let him know how you feel or to make it 'better', must be resisted. Once your son realizes that he has your full attention and that you are not going to hijack the conversation, his pauses and silences will evaporate (except occasionally to give him time to order his thoughts), and he will be calmer and more focused. Listening without interrupting is not to say that you approve of all that is being said, but this is not the time to step in and correct – that comes later. Often we fill the gaps because we are tense or cannot bear to hear what is being said, rather than as a positive response to your son's tension.

I solve my problems for myself and then I go to the person who will give me the advice I want to hear.
Twenty-year-old

If you want to signal during the conversation that you understand, use simple, low-key responses that are unobtrusive and will not interrupt your son's train of thought. Encouraging nods, facial expressions, and other non-verbal gestures can be enough to show that you are listening and you have understood.

Also watch out for the common male trait of turning the conversation into a joke just as he gets close to the nub of the problem. It is a defensive mechanism that boys use to make light of their difficulties. Do not allow him to deflect your interest and concern by cracking a glib one-liner. Instead, try to keep him focused and return to the crucial part of what he is saying.

Reflective listening

Reflective listening is a tool frequently used by therapists and counsellors to encourage troubled children to talk about what is on their mind, particularly when they are distressed. This listening technique does not use questions, it simply uses acknowledging statements to tell the talker, using his own words, what the listener hears him saying, and how he appears to be feeling. Effectively, you summarize the gist of what your child has said to let them know you have understood and you are feeding it back to him so that he can focus his mind on what is troubling him and move on.

Here is a brief example:

Parent: You look like you've had a rotten day.
Son: Yeah.
Parent: Sounds like you aren't keen to talk about it right now.
Son: You'll probably just shout at me like all the others.
Parent: You don't want to talk about it because you're worried I might shout at you too.

Son: Yeah, I hate Mr Fellows. He's always shouting at me without listening to my side of the story.
Parent: Mr Fellows doesn't listen to you but you'd like me to.
Son: Yes, it's not fair because so-and-so did such-and-such …

And his story spills out.

This form of listening is non-judgemental and encourages a child to tell you what is really happening, rather than what they think you want to hear.

Reflective listening can be broken down into two important elements. First, succinctly reflect back what your child has said so that he knows you understand. The second phase involves feeding back underlying emotions, which is slightly more speculative since you have to briefly describe what you imagine he may be experiencing. For instance:

Son: I was the only one in Newcastle United kit. Everyone else was wearing Sunderland.
Parent: Sounds like you felt excluded.
Son: Yeah, and Alex said I was a rubbish striker.
Parent: I guess you've had better days.
Son: Oh it wasn't so bad. At least I scored a goal. That shut him up!

As you can see, there are lots of phrases like, 'It sounds like', 'I guess', 'I suspect', and 'I imagine'. Avoid comments such as 'I know just what you're feeling', because you could be very wide of the mark and you will draw their derision if you are wrong. Using the previous example, the conversation could have taken a very different turn if you had stated rather than suggested how your son was feeling:

Son: I was the only one in Newcastle United kit. Everyone else was wearing Sunderland.
Parent: I bet you wish you'd had a Sunderland strip.
Son: No way, Newcastle are way better than Sunderland! We're the best. Don't you know anything about football?

There will be occasions when you do not have the faintest notion what your son is talking about, let alone what he is feeling. If this is the case, be honest and simply ask him. Expressions such as 'I don't know what that must have felt like ...' or 'Let me see if I've got this right ...' are much better than pretending you know exactly how he feels, and may help him to make sense of his emotions as he relates them to you. Once he has achieved this, it is much easier for him to let those feelings go.

However, there are a couple of pitfalls with 'reflective listening'. Firstly, it is not a technique to use haphazardly. It was developed by therapists to help children work out their feelings and what has happened to them. If you use it with ubiquitous abandon in everyday situations, you trivialize it and may end up with egg on your face.

> If your parents react badly, you won't tell them anything else. You're more likely to talk if someone will listen and not punish you.   *Fourteen-year-old*

Son: Can you get off the rocking chair?
Parent: Get off the rocking chair? Sounds like you don't want me around at the moment.
Son: No, it's on my foot!

Use reflective listening sparingly and at the appropriate time, and it will work for you.

The second pitfall is that 'reflective listening' is not an easy technique to master, but many professionals and parents sing its praises. Most proponents of this technique admit that you feel foolish when you first start to use it and that it does not come naturally. Indeed your son will probably notice and may even comment on your new style of speech, probably in a derogatory or sarcastic way. However, experts recommend that if you stick with it, it will feel like second nature after a few weeks and it will definitely reap benefits. If it still does not work for you after six to eight weeks, it is probably not the best technique for you and your family.

'Reflective listening is just a technique and it can only complement an intention, which is to provide quality listening in order to really get to know and understand your child,' says Dr Dinah Jayson, a child and adolescent consultant psychiatrist at the Trafford Trust. She uses

---

Parents make assumptions, and they still say the same things. They have a programmed response. They always give a common response.

Eighteen-year-old

---

reflective listening in her clinical work and with her three children, and says,

> 'It helps you really understand where your child is com-
> ing from and why he. acts and feels as he does. The
> messages it conveys if you really mean what you are
> saying are, "I am here for you come what may," and "You
> are more important to me than other distractions and I'll
> make special time just for you." Or maybe, "I won't com-
> ment or give advice unless asked. I just want to see your
> side of things" which is especially potent and hard to do
> if your son knows that you disagree on something.'

She recommends that you do not worry too much about technique, but simply make sure that you really try to see it his way, and then you can tentatively check out some of these ideas if you think you are beginning to understand.

■ PROBLEM SOLVING
Are you a good listener?
We all like to pride ourselves on being a good listener, but often we are not listening as well as we might. Com-edy sketches abound about sympathetic friends looking concerned while one recounts her tale of woe, only to be dismissed by a, 'Yeah, yeah, how awful, now listen to me' riposte. Unwittingly, as parents, we often do this, and worse, to our kids. Here are some of the common banana skins that slip up the unwary listener:

Solving it for him
Son: I can't find my homework book and it has to be in today.

Parent: Simply tell Mrs Watkins that you've misplaced it and can you have another copy and you'll hand it in tomorrow.

Being dismissive
Son: George has broken my favourite pencil.
Parent: Never mind, we'll get you another one.

Patronizing
Son: She's always touching my things.
Parent: Yes, but you've always been so good at sharing.

Being smug or critical
Son: Mrs Higson has confiscated my Pokemon cards.
Parent: Well, I told you not to take them to school.

Giving reassurance
Son: I'm scared of the dark.
Parent: There's nothing to be afraid of. The dark won't hurt you.

Diversionary
Son: No one wanted to play with me at school today.
Parent: Well, you come and play Scrabble with me. That's much more fun.

Correcting
Son: Why can't I have one of them biscuits? Alex has had two.
Parent: It's those biscuits, not them.
Finally, worst of all:

Ignoring
Son: I really want to go to the rugby on Saturday but there's no one to take me.
Parent: Did you say sausages or pizza?

Most parents fall into the trap of using these closed responses to a lesser or greater degree some of the time – after all, we are only human. Unfortunately, if used all the time, they simply prevent your son from talking to you, whereas the real purpose of being a good listener is to encourage him to talk.

■ PROBLEM SOLVING
My son can't open up
Sometimes your natural instincts tell you that something is troubling your child, but he's not opening up to you. Treading the fine line between respecting his privacy and making yourself available to talk is not easy, but you have to take the initiative and give it a go.

Look for openings in his general conversation or for clues. Sometimes youngsters who cannot ask for your help outright may leave a letter or postcard or something for you to find that raises the issue.

You could always be upfront and simply say that you are concerned about him and ask if there is anything wrong. You may get an indignant denial but, on the other hand, this might just be the opening your son has been waiting for. If your overture is rejected, try not to take it personally, and just back off for a while. If it is a problem that he has been wrestling with, he may come back to you later that day or some time soon, now he knows that you are there for him if he needs help.

If he does decide to confide in you, you have to be prepared to hear anything he has to say, however unpalatable it is for you. If you are to have a safe and open relationship with your son, he must be able to tell you about anything – often the most important things our sons have to tell us are the hardest things for them to say. Obviously, you do not have to agree or approve of what you hear and you can always take action later, but while he is confiding in you, your job is to listen and not to jump to conclusions or pronounce judgements.

Finally, when the boot is on the other foot and something is troubling you, you should try not to feel that you must always protect your children from unpleasant news or truths. Your children are more perceptive than you imagine and they will sense if there is something wrong in the home. Although it may be difficult for you to discuss problems with your son, it may lessen family tension if you air your troubles.

Getting him to listen
Now you have got your son to open up. However, to quote an old cliché, communication is a two-way street and it is just as important for your son to listen as well as talk. If you communicate well in the normal course of events, there is every hope that when the chips are down, you will be able to discuss problems together.

What you can do
In reality, your son will learn to listen if he feels you listen to him. However, there is quite a lot you can do to increase

the chances of getting through to your son, even in everyday, ordinary circumstances.

> You don't think your parents have been through it.
> *Seventeen-year-old*

- *Use appropriate language.* If what you say and how you say it is far too complex for your son's level of understanding, he will probably switch off. Keep it simple.
- *Keep to the point.* It is so easy to fall into the trap of wittering on, particularly if you feel that your son has not been responding fast enough or paying attention. However, talking non-stop about his failings will simply go way over his head. Stick to the point rather than get into the 'and another thing …' scenario.
- *One thing at a time.* If you overwhelm your son with a flood of information or instructions, there is every chance that your requests will be lost in a sea of words and he will end up doing nothing. Concentrate on one thing at a time and you will stand a better chance of your request registering.
- *Pick your moment.* Asking your son to do something two minutes before the end of the FA Cup final or in the middle of a furious argument is unlikely to get results. In fact, he probably will not take the slightest notice of what you say if you get your timing horribly wrong.
- *Close proximity matters.* We all do it, but shouting from the other room is not going to get results. It is

much better to stand in the room with him and speak quietly but firmly.

- *Do not speak across each other.* There is generally so much going on in the average family home that everyone talks at once, and several conversations are held at the same time. If you want your children to take heed, make sure you get into the habit of granting each person time to speak. No one will take the time to listen if you are constantly being drowned out by a louder member of the family.

- *Use your son's name.* You are far more likely to get your child's attention if you simply say his name before you speak to him – a useful teachers' tip.

- *Watch your words.* Although all children have selective hearing, do not confuse not listening with not hearing. Any conversation within your son's earshot will be picked up on, especially if it is about him, so watch what you say.

- *Mean what you say.* All kids recognize when 'five minutes only' means that and when it means a good twenty minutes more play because the parent is engrossed in whatever he or she is doing. Your body language and non-verbal messages should match what you are saying, otherwise you fool no one.

- *Check that the message has been received.* This is not to be confused with the 'What did I just say?' approach, which is usually a reprimand when you are pretty certain that what you just said has gone in one ear and out the other. If you have given an instruction or made an arrangement, give yourself

> **Boys' hearing**
> Stephen Biddulph, author and psychologist, explains in his book, *Raising Boys* (HarperCollins, 1998) that boys experience explosive growth spurts at various times. During these bouts, their ear canals stretch and thin, and can easily be blocked, giving them temporary deafness. There is no way of knowing when this might affect a child, but your son may not be pretending not to hear you or ignoring you, he could be experiencing a real, albeit temporary, loss of hearing.

peace of mind by asking, 'Can I check what we've agreed here?'

■ PROBLEM SOLVING
My teenage son lies to me

It is an unpalatable fact that children, and teenagers in particular, lie to their parents. Usually, it is over small things, such as the details of where they are going and what they are going to do. Worse still, when caught out in a wrongdoing they may persist in telling a bare-faced lie, even if the facts are undeniable.

Given that most parents believe that their relationship with their son should be founded on trust, this can come as quite a blow. However, it should not – because virtually all teenagers do it. And if we are honest, we may have lied to our parents and it did not necessarily make us into dishonest adults.

This is not to say you have to condone it just because it goes on – lying should be challenged. Nevertheless, it is more important that you do not lose sight of the issue about which your son is lying. If your son swears blind that he told you about an important meeting at school concerning falling grades and he patently did not, the big issue is the fact that he is failing in school, rather than that he lied. If you focus on the lying, you could miss the more immediate and important issue.

What you can do
- ***Keep things in perspective.*** It would be nice to think you can trust your son, but do not be fooled into thinking that your relationship with him is irretrievably damaged because he has lied to you.
- ***Always confront deceit.*** Never let a lie pass without showing your displeasure and upset, but remember that however deplorable deceit may be, it is normal teenage behaviour.
- ***Being trusted is important to your son's self-esteem.*** 'You can trust me. I'm not a child any more' is what he may say, but do not be deluded into believing it entirely. Without letting on to him, expect some deviousness and sneaking around, and be prepared for it.
- ***Realize that you can trust him in certain areas and not in others.*** Allow him greater freedom in areas where he has proved trustworthy, and be more circumspect in areas where he has previously let you down.
- ***Do not be blackmailed.*** If your son feels he has the slightest chance of getting away with it, he will lie. If

you say that you do not believe him, he will become incandescent with righteous indignation, whether he is telling the truth or not. In a teenager's mind, you should believe him unquestioningly (despite the evidence) because he feels he deserves your trust. Do not feel bad about challenging him just because of his self-righteous rage over your accusations.

- *Do not confuse lying to parents with being a liar.* Teenagers have a strange double standard, according to which it is okay to lie to your parents. This is an aspect of the game of 'getting away with it' that is part and parcel of growing independence. He will not see it as immoral and you should not believe that it indicates that he will be a pathological liar as an adult.

- *Lead by example.* It is that old chestnut again. Of course, you can be cross with a son who lies and you may decide to punish him, but the only effective way to teach your son not to lie is to practise honesty yourself.

■ CASE STUDY – Dan's story

'I suppose you would say that I'm quite an open, touchy-feely person in the first place, which is probably why I was prepared to give reflective listening a go.

'I have always been very hands-on with the raising of the kids and I feel I have a good relationship with all my children. I was aware of the importance of good communication having been through therapy myself to deal with issues about my own background. I was so determined that the boys were not going to suffer like me that I kept asking them to tell me how they were feeling, and if they were okay. It used to enrage me that, despite my frequent enquiries, they wouldn't open up to me. If anything, I think it made them clam up more.

'A friend told me about reflective listening and, after reading up about it, I decided to introduce it into our family. At first, the boys obviously thought I was nuts. "Dad's lost it this time," was the general consensus. I must admit I felt a bit of a lemon repeating their words back to them and it didn't feel natural at all. But I stuck at it.

'I think once I became less self-conscious about talking in this way, then the boys relaxed a bit too. I was amazed the first time I got a response. Isaac simply told me about an unfortunate incident at school and I could scarcely believe my ears. I was so stunned that he'd told me that I didn't comment – which is probably the best approach.

'Looking back, I realized that in my eagerness to get the boys to communicate, I used to virtually interrogate them about how they were feeling, and I would tell them what I thought they must be going through. No wonder they wouldn't tell me things – what a pompous ass.

'I probably used reflective listening techniques too much at the beginning because I was so keen. It now comes quite easily to me but I only use it when I feel it is appropriate. The boys no longer comment on my strange speech so it must sound more natural to them as well. It has certainly made a difference to our communication. I find it particularly useful in calming down our younger son when he's in a rage. Before, just trying to speak to him seemed to escalate the crisis but feeding back what he's saying, showing that I'm listening, and letting him know that he's going to be heard seems to have a remarkably calming effect.'

Dealing with feelings

On the weight of evidence so far, it seems that:

- Boys equate manliness with stoicism and self-reliance.
- Boys do not want to burden family and friends with their feelings.
- Due to social conditioning, boys do not show their emotions, to the extent that some deny they even experience any.

It is small wonder that boys can be so out of touch and unforthcoming about how they feel. The obvious solution to this perennial problem that has undoubtedly struck every sensitive and progressive parent, is to encourage your son to talk to you, as we saw in Chapter Six.

Blokes give other blokes appeasement (pacification) and then go out for drinks and move on mentally.

Nineteen-year-old

However, there is one fatal flaw in this plan: boys cannot talk about what they do not fully understand. Moreover, they often lack the vocabulary to express themselves. They have what is now commonly known in educational circles as emotional illiteracy.

Studies show that mothers (who spend the predominant amount of time with their children) are more likely to talk about emotions with daughters, and tend to stick to discussing facts with sons, even when they are toddlers. If your son cannot recognize, let alone express, what he is experiencing, he may react to stress in the only way he knows, namely emotional withdrawal or anger, and possibly violence.

Therefore, before you can get your son to talk about what he is experiencing, you have to give him the tools to do so.

Getting in touch
As with many aspects of parenting, the best way to help your son to recognize and express his feelings is to lead by example. If you take time to share with him how you feel and allow him to see your emotions, he will learn that this is not only acceptable but healthy. It is particularly useful for fathers or important men in a boy's life to guide by showing how they handle their feelings. Research shows that if fathers are silent on the subject of their emotions or relationships, sons believe that this is how men should behave.

> It's difficult to know who to talk to. Your dad's probably suffering from the same em otional suppression because that's probably how his father dealt with things – by not saying anything. *Eighteen-year-old*

If boys see only women being emotional there is a danger that they may dismiss this behaviour as yet another exclusively female trait or, put another way, a non-male characteristic, and so steer clear of it. Naturally, predominantly female households can still lead by example, but it helps if there is some male support.

'Discussing emotions in everyday conversation can help build emotional literacy,' says Dr Dinah Jayson, a childhood adolescent consultant psychiatrist at the Trafford Trust. 'For example, if he tells you a friend lost his temper, you can ask, "How do you think he was feeling? What made him so upset?" and this can lead on to more general conversations about feeling upset, and how to deal with it. So you can ask him how he thinks his friend handled the situation and what other strategies he thinks could have helped,' she adds.

However, the flip side of encouraging your son to be in touch with his feelings is that you must not be surprised when he lets his emotions out. It is no good encouraging your son to express himself, if you then tell him in a stage whisper 'not to make a fuss' when he gets upset, particularly if it is in public. In fact, you may find that genuine upset is usually reserved for when he feels he is in a safe haven, more often than not at home, and that public histrionics have some quite different hidden agenda. You will soon get adept at spotting what is real and what is phoney.

> I wouldn't tell a friend [about my problems] unless I was absolutely certain he would keep it secret.
>
> *Sixteen-year-old*

> Being upset must not be in the public domain.
>
> *Fifteen-year-old*

Furthermore, it is worth remembering that by encouraging your son to express how he feels, you are flying in the face of convention. You may be laying him open to ridicule and derision from his less-enlightened friends if he bares his soul in their company. For this reason, many parents point out the realities of life to their sons and explain that although there are no barriers to showing his feelings at home, he may prefer to save face with his mates, and keep his feelings to himself. Sadly, this perpetuates the 'stiff upper lip' cycle for boys, yet it is understandable that parents want to protect their child from emotional hurt.

Incidentally, if you tell your son that home is a safe haven for self-expression, you must be prepared for all emotions, not just the ones with which you are comfortable. Depending on your upbringing, you may find expressions of anger acutely discomforting or being sad unacceptable. Many parents are highly uncomfortable if their son says, 'I hate so-and-so', especially if it is a sibling. Nevertheless hurriedly saying, 'You don't really mean that' is not necessarily the right approach. Suppressing or denying the expression of an emotion does not eliminate what your son is feeling.

> Parents are over-concerned whereas friends know when to stop and back off. You want to sit back and solve the problem for yourself. *Seventeen-year-old*

Acknowledging your son's feelings may be all he needs to start dealing with them.

By the same token, if from his earliest years you have told your son not to feel how he feels, he may stop telling you. And, if he denies his emotions for long enough, eventually he may lose confidence in his ability to recognize his own feelings, making them less easy to deal with, and making him more susceptible to influence by others.

As an infant, you are naturally uninhibited in expressing what you feel but you learn to suppress and control your feelings, and keep them from your parents, according to the culture in which you live. In our society, parents are normally quite good at responding to their children's positive emotions, such as joy and pride in an achievement and, within reason, they are there for them when they are down. Yet how you respond to your son when he expresses negative emotions such as anger, jealousy or fear can strongly influence his sense of self-worth.

Identifying emotions

It is never too late, but the sooner your son can start labelling emotions, the better. Giving specific names to emotions is very effective in helping children to identify, acknowledge, and deal with how they are feeling.

Younger children (or if this is a new exercise for an older child) benefit from some adult help in working out how they feel, even though it may feel alien to you at first. This is where reflective listening (see Chapter Six) can come into its own. Comments in everyday situations, such as 'You seem perhaps a bit excited and a bit scared?' before going on a ride at Alton Towers, can introduce the idea of discussing feelings as well

> It takes me a while to recognize what I'm feeling and
> then I can express it.   *Eighteen-year-old*

as facts into your son's life. In this way, you can gently broaden their vocabulary to reflect the full gamut of their emotions.

The fact that you have recognized and seem to understand what he is feeling is enormously reassuring and beneficial to your child, even if you do not agree with the reasons why.

In addition, it is important to let him know that while his feelings are valid, that does not give him carte blanche to express them in any way he likes. It is up to you to let him know what behaviour is acceptable and what is beyond the pale. For example, you can understand his frustration at not being picked for the team, but screaming at you on the touchline is not going to alter his selection, nor does it help him or you.

Recognizing and understanding what he is feeling is not the same as putting up with how he reacts. If you do not like his behaviour, tell him so, and ask him to find a better way to respond. If he is so swept up in the power of his emotions that he cannot think straight, you can suggest alternative ways of behaving that may help him (and indirectly you) to cope. It is of enormous benefit to boys in particular to realize that they have a choice in how they communicate their emotions and that the age-old recourse to anger and violence is not the only option.

Boys in particular have difficulty discussing their emotions per se. If you ask your son why he behaved in a certain fashion after an angry outburst, he may clam up. Thus, emotions are best discussed when externalized. For instance, rather than asking him, 'You madman! What the hell did you do x, y and z for?' you are more likely to get an honest answer if you remove the blame. Instead, you may say, 'You were in the grip of anger when you did x, y and z.' You can go on to explain how anger is an external force that makes you do daft things that can lead to trouble and misery. Then he is better able to objectively discuss what caused the feelings that led to his angry eruption. Now, before you dismiss this technique as one that simply absolves him of all responsibility for his actions, you can still make it clear that you disapprove. However, you do so by attacking the behaviour, not him personally.

Nonetheless, it is worth reflecting that anger is rarely productively discussed when someone is in its clutches. It is better to have these discussions with your son in his calmer moments or once the storm has abated if you are talking about a specific incident.

Externalizing emotions is a technique used to excellent effect in clinical situations, and it can be of great benefit to parents. If you can persuade your son to see anger or any other negative emotion as an external force, he can fight it by catching it out. He can spot the times before 'anger' sneaks up on him and be prepared for it. Boys relate very well to seeing things as good versus evil, light against dark. If he can see himself as a Jeddi knight fighting the dark force of anger, an emotional warrior if you like, he may be able to use positive thought to fight his negative emotional responses. There is nothing remotely weak about this technique and, if it allows your son to stop and think before acting rashly or angrily, it is making him stronger and safer.

■ PROBLEM SOLVING
My son is depressed
Adolescence is a time of highs and lows and most teenagers will exhibit mood swings at some time or another. Girls tend to suffer more periods of intense gloom than boys, but when life is difficult or disappointing both sexes can appear morose and angst-ridden.

Creative emotion
If your son finds it difficult to identify and name his emotions, some parents have found that sharing books and stories can help younger children to explore the feelings of others which, in turn, can help them to recognize and understand their own emotions.

However, if your son is past the age of sharing stories, ask him to express how he feels in a painting or drawing. However, I recommend that you wait until an angry outburst has calmed down before making this suggestion or you may find that his ideas for what you can do with your paint brush are a little offensive!

If he agrees, you may be surprised by what he produces – sometimes kids use graphic symbols or images when they do not have the vocabulary or the confidence to express themselves in words. This creative medium helps to reinforce the message that even negative emotions can be expressed without aggression.

Fortunately, most young people are extremely resilient and, before you know it, they have passed through these periods of gloom as they come to terms with whatever was bothering them.

Nevertheless, for a few youngsters, their misery persists much longer than you might reasonably expect, sometimes long after the apparent cause has disappeared. Their low state of mind impacts on all aspects of their lives, adversely affecting friendships, schoolwork, social life, and family relationships.

Research suggests that 3–6 per cent of fourteen- to sixteen-year-olds suffer from true depressive illness and depression is rare in children under the age of nine. Depressive illness is also twice as likely to affect women than men.

Not only are there more than 2 million children attending doctors' surgeries with some form of psychological or emotional problem, but there are 19,000 suicide attempts by adolescents every year – more than one every thirty minutes. Add to that the study by the Mental Health Foundation called *Bright Futures: Promoting Children and Young People's Mental Health* published in June 1999, which concludes that children are becoming less resilient and less able to cope with the ups and downs of life, and it is unsurprising that parents are concerned.

It would be clear with very good friends if they were very low and I would be able to know the reasons why.

Twenty-year-old

Why are so many teenagers depressed? At a time when they are trying to establish their identity and their brains are exposed to great hormonal fluctuations, teenagers are surrounded by images of what they should be. They are under pressure to perform well at school, to look good, to have the latest clothes, mobile phones, and IT (information technology). On top of that they may be worried about drugs, bullying, their parents' divorce, and sex. It is understandable that there is a virtual epidemic of teenage depression. Depression is not always due to information overload and stress, but can often be related to events or sad experiences, such as family breakdown or the death of a loved one. Neglect, abuse, and bullying can all trigger depression, and teenagers are more likely to become depressed if they feel they have no one to share their worries with. In some cases, depression can be genetic and anyone with a close relative who suffers from depression has a higher than normal risk of becoming depressed themselves. Whatever the cause of depression, all the evidence shows that early intervention is vital. A recent US study in the *Journal of American Medicine* shows that if depression is not caught early, teenagers may end up as depressed adults, and a significant number of those will attempt suicide.

If your son is consistently miserable, withdrawn, and depressed, and this lasts for more than two or three weeks, you may have cause for concern.

How to spot a depressed teenager
According to the charity, YoungMinds, it is important to know the difference between teenage blues and serious depression. If your teenager has experienced three or more of the

following symptoms and has felt like it for more than two weeks, go and see your doctor or contact one of the organizations listed below.

- Complaints of boredom.
- Low energy and feeling tired all the time.
- Nothing feels good any more.
- Lack of interest in food or overeating.
- Loss of interest in school or friends.
- Irritability, agitation and uncharacteristic outbursts of anger or aggression.
- Great anxiety.
- No interest in normal social/sporting activities.
- Decrease in self-care.
- Sleeping too much or too little.
- Requesting frequent days off school.
- Difficulty concentrating.
- Feeling guilty about things.
- Feeling life is pointless.
- Lack of sex drive.
- Tearfulness.

What you can do
As much as you may want to help your son yourself, if he is truly under the influence of depression, you cannot do it alone. He needs to seek professional help – preferably your family doctor who may prescribe antidepressants. However, the first-line treatment for youngsters (provided that the waiting list is not too long) is usually some kind of psychological treatment – either counselling or psychotherapy. Yet how on earth do you persuade a depressed and reluctant

adolescent to visit your doctor, let alone a psychologist or psychiatrist?

- Most professionals recommend that you approach the problem as a family problem, and make this clear to your son.
- Explain that you desperately want to help but you do not think that you are able to do so alone.
- Point out that no one is to blame, that you also feel responsible but that it is a situation that cannot be resolved by yourselves.
- Sometimes, a trusted outsider, such as a teacher or coach who is emotionally distanced from the family, can be more successful in persuading a depressed teenager to talk or seek help.
- Contact the Depression Alliance (tel: 020 7633 0557) for a copy of their booklet, *The Young Person's Guide to Stress*, or call the YoungMinds Parents Information Service (tel: 0800 018 2138).
- Try giving him St John's Wort. A recent German study of a hundred teenagers with mild to moderate depressive symptoms taking the herbal remedy showed that, after two weeks, 76 per cent of doctors rated the effects of the supplement as 'good or excellent' with 97 per cent saying that after four weeks children were vastly improved.
- If your son agrees that outside help is required, make an appointment with your doctor.
- Keep calm and take things one step at a time, i.e. don't start worrying about how to get him to a counsellor before you've even got him to the doctor, for example.

Dealing with emotions

All human beings experience emotions as a specific set of body sensations in response to certain situations. Some people feel these emotions more strongly than others, but we all experience them.

There are four dominant emotions, namely anger, sadness, fear, and joy, and the rest of our feelings are a combination of these. Thus, jealousy is anger with a dab of fear; if you feel wistful, you are probably experiencing a mixture of sadness and joy, and so on.

Just like you, your children will find themselves in situations that produce these (for them) unfamiliar feelings, and the only clues they have about how to handle these strange feelings are construed from what they see happening around them – that is to say, principally you. Therefore, if you handle your anger by flying into a red-faced rage, then guess what? Your child will see that as the norm and follow suit.

Now, rather than suggest that you should never get cross or raise your voice, there are ways in which you can teach your children by example how to experience and manage the three negative emotions productively:

Anger

When a child feels angry, his natural response is to lash out. This is virtually an inbred reflex action but, in the modern world, it is not very useful, and you have to show your son alternative ways to express his anger.

There are plenty of things that can make adults want to resort to violence too (think of road- or air-rage), but you have to moderate your behaviour to survive in a modern society.

Consequently, you learn to express your anger loudly and with conviction, but also with control. If you have no anger, you leave yourself open to being pushed around, and this is not what you want for your son. Too much anger, and he may get labelled a bully. To get the balance right, you should help him from the earliest years to practise the following techniques to manage his anger:

- Help him to think of anger as an external force that he is able to battle and overcome.
- When in the grip of anger, encourage him to stop and think, to calm down – counting to ten really does work – and then to consider his options and their consequences, and to choose the best one.
- Encourage him to use words to express how he feels and allow him to say out loud that he is feeling very angry. However, do not accept violence whatever the provocation.
- Help him to trace back to find the cause of his anger. Often an outburst is as inexplicable to him as it is to you but by giving him some suggestions, he may be able to identify the cause.
- Acknowledge his feelings. This will not always change whatever it is that he has taken exception to, but it will help if he knows that his feelings are heard and understood.
- Train him to use his anger positively. Give him the vocabulary to ask for things forcefully and to stand up for himself without losing control.
- Show him that when you are angry, you are still in control. There is no harm in telling your kids loudly

and clearly when and why you are cross, but try to make sure that you are in control and that you are able to let it go afterwards (sulking is anger and sadness mixed for effect and it is very negative). Never resort to abuse or belittling your son when you are angry, stick to the facts.

- If you witness your son struggling to show some restraint, praise him and encourage him, for example, 'You fought that anger really well by not allowing your sister to bait you.' After all, there are plenty of adults who never master this skill, so any steps in the right direction should be acknowledged.

- To keep on the straight and narrow, suggest he uses affirmations. For example, 'I can fight my temper. I'm stronger than it and it won't get the better of me', 'Temper leads to trouble and I want fun, not trouble' or 'I'm getting stronger every day'.

Sadness

Sadness is one of the toughest emotions for a boy to try to handle. From their earliest years, it is drummed into boys that if you cry too much, you are a crybaby and, as they get older, that it is weak to cry.

Nonetheless, it is proven that expressing your emotions is good for you and conversely, that bottling up your sadness makes you uptight and brittle. If you want your son to be a strong man, the best thing you can do to help him is to show him how to handle sadness instead of suppressing it.

> When you move into your teens, there's an expectation that you don't cry and you should be in control and, if there's a problem, then lads should be able to handle it. That's quite useful if you become a fireman or something and you can deal with an emergency unemotionally, and then deal with the emotions afterwards but it doesn't translate too well into civvy street where boys are trying to deal with emotions they don't understand. *Twenty-year-old*

- Again, teach by example. Do not try to keep your tears hidden from your son. Letting him see your sadness is not the same as falling to pieces in front of his very eyes, but telling him that grown-ups get sad too can help him to accept sadness as a normal and acceptable feeling.
- Tell him that it is okay to cry. Use situations such as the death of a pet to explain that some things are worth feeling sad about.
- Be there for him when he is sad. Just being present is enormously comforting but take your lead from him. Sometimes he might want to be held but sometimes he may only want to be near you.
- After listening to him, reassure him that his sadness will pass in time.

Fear

Boys especially need to know that fear is an acceptable and necessary emotion. In a culture where bravery is deemed cool and equates to manliness, boys often believe that to be fearless is highly desirable.

Nevertheless, it is fear that keeps you safe. That cautionary nag in your ear before you do something foolhardy or downright dangerous is the early warning system that we all possess and your son should heed it. After disaster has struck, during gap-year travels for example, it is too late for your son to turn around and say, 'I had a funny feeling things weren't all above board with that bungee-jumping firm!'

Of course, we are preaching to the converted since nearly every parent spends their days trying to get their son to be less reckless. Yet getting your son to accept that fear is essential to survival – fear of danger and nowadays fear of the over-solicitous stranger or hostile street situation – is an important message.

Naturally, being too fearful is also a handicap – all children need to be brave enough to try new experiences, to speak up for themselves or to make new friends. It is important that fear of failure should not prevent your son from experiencing life to the full.

After all, just the right amount of fear can be good. It is energizing – it can lift a sporting performance, pre-performance nerves can produce the concert of a lifetime, and there is nothing like fear to focus the mind. Funny how coming face to face with a savage dog puts pay to idle day-dreaming.

Explain to your son that far from making him pathetic, having a little fear in his life will protect him. It may help him to handle his fears if you:

- **Acknowledge his fears.** Travelling to France alone on an exchange for the first time is pretty daunting, so acknowledge this fact. This will make him more emotionally resilient and better able to cope.

- *Do not ridicule his fears.* Even gentle teasing can be upsetting to a son who has struggled to express a very real anxiety. Remember, it takes courage for a boy to admit that he is scared of abseiling, for example.

- *Raise his self-esteem generally.* If your son is excessively fearful about everything, do what you can. Encourage him to discuss situations that trouble him (concentrating on one at a time), and to come up with ways to overcome his fears.

- *Encourage him to think through dangerous situations.* Consider threats from bullying, abduction, abuse, and ask him to come up with a plan. Use 'what if' scenarios to get him thinking and talking.

- *Help him to externalize his fear to make it controllable.* Ask him to visualize his fear in a physical form. Then picture that manifestation in a particularly humorous or ridiculous situation. When he is able to laugh at it (his fear), he can mentally flick it away in a puff of smoke. This externalization technique is used to good effect in family therapy sessions, and can be used whenever he finds himself in a fearful situation.

- *Trust your son's intuitive sense of fear.* And allow him to believe in it too. If he feels cautious about a certain person or is uneasy in a given situation, trust his instincts and support him. Fear is your protective radar that rarely lets you down.

The danger of labelling

Helping your child to label his emotions is useful, but labelling him by using expressions such as 'clumsy clot', 'thoughtless boy', and 'clever lad' is not.

However, it is something that many parents do because this is how they were raised. Using a label can give you a similar feeling to swearing – exclaiming 'You stupid boy!' when he spills the milk brings an immediate emotional release that makes you feel momentarily better, and perversely is considered better than saying 'Oh bloody hell'. Yet labels can be self-fulfilling and a boy who is repeatedly told that he is 'spiteful' will believe the label, and act accordingly.

Even positive labels can be damaging. Sayings such as 'You are such a brave boy' or 'You are the clever one' can lead to resentment, and to feelings that they have to live up to expectations or that the love they receive is conditional on them maintaining their 'label' status.

Like adults, children do not like to be value judged and labelling can make a child even less keen to cooperate. How can you get out of the habit of using labels that you say so easily?

Firstly, it is important to separate the doer from the deed. Criticize the behaviour or act rather than the perpetrator, which means avoiding phrases like 'You're so clumsy' and saying instead, 'Your room's a mess' or 'That was unkind'.

While still concentrating on the behaviour, give as much information as possible. Therefore, rather than shouting 'You clumsy idiot', state that he has 'got ketchup on the table cloth which now needs washing'. This may feel like you are 'stating the obvious', but to a young person who is often unsure of why his parents are flying off the handle, it is very useful.

Young boys are known to cooperate more if they understand the effects of their behaviour, and if they do not feel threatened.

If you extend this technique to explain how actions can affect other people and their feelings, you are/making him more socially aware. An awareness of how his actions can impinge on others can have a positive effect in the battle against bullying, racism, and sexism.

■ PROBLEM SOLVING
My son is suicidal

Although you may think this is something that happens to other families, be aware that the suicide rate among fifteen- to twenty-four-year-old men in the UK rose by 85 per cent between 1980 and 1990, and is now the second most common cause of death amongst this age group. A NCH (National Children's Home) Action for Children fact file 2000 points out that the high rate among young men may be related to increased fears of unemployment, alcohol/drug misuse, and parental marital breakdown.

Very often the trigger for a suicide attempt is a discipline issue where the youngster is afraid that he is about to be found out about truanting or some trouble with the police, for example. Strangely enough, he does not wait until there is a huge family bust-up, but becomes suicidal at the thought of an impending row over some behaviour or misdemeanour of which he is ashamed. Perhaps it follows the break-up of a relationship. Whatever the cause, most parents are horrified to discover that their child has been miserable enough to contemplate or attempt suicide, and they have been unaware of his desolation.

The one positive aspect is that most suicide attempts fail, and that youngsters often flag up their intent in various ways. Nonetheless, if your son has tried to take his life once or talked about suicide, then he is vulnerable, and some form of professional counselling is needed straight away.

Signs to look out for
Parents of children who have attempted suicide generally agree that, with the benefit of hindsight, they remember changes in their children's behaviour in the days leading to the attempt. Some of the more common signs include:

- Becomes withdrawn and isolated from friends. Has difficulty sleeping and does not eat well.
- Struggles to talk about or explain his feelings.
- Schoolwork deteriorates markedly.
- Seems overwhelmed by school/exam pressure.
- Is generally very tearful and despondent.
- Takes unnecessary risks – perhaps drives recklessly, drinks too much or takes drugs.
- Appears overwhelmed by life's difficulties – a relationship break-up, trouble at school, brushes with the law.
- Has a disturbing interest in ways and means of committing suicide, i.e. asking about what happens if you throw yourself under a train, how many pills you have to take, etc.
- Occasionally makes statements such as 'I wish I were dead' or 'My life's rubbish and I've got nothing to live for'. An American study, 'Your Child's Development From Birth to Adolescence', showed that 42 per cent of teenagers who attempted or actually committed

suicide had previously spoken of having serious suicidal thoughts.

If your son exhibits any of the above risk factors, take heed and seek immediate help to lift him from his despair.

What you can do as a precaution
- Encourage your son to talk to you generally about his feelings and especially if you suspect that he feels miserable.
- However half-hearted, never dismiss talk of suicide or a poor attempt as 'attention seeking' – your child needs care and professional attention if he feels this desperate.
- Help your child to identify, name and understand his feelings so that he is better able to cope with life's crises.
- Do not put too much pressure on your son at exam time. Research suggests that a young lad who believes that his academic success falls short of his parents' expectations is vulnerable to suicidal thoughts.
- Consider replacing paracetemol tablets in the medicine cabinet with aspirin or ibuprofen – it only takes twenty paracetemol tablets to cause fatal liver failure several days after a suicide attempt. If a desperate teenager swallows a handful of pills as a gesture, he could die by mistake if he chooses the wrong tablets.
- Do not leave medication lying around. Lock it away and buy medication in blister packs rather than in bottles – the delay in taking the tablets may be enough to deter him from taking an overdose on impulse.

Although suicidal tendencies can be spotted in some cases, on occasion there are no warning signs, and nothing could have been done to predict or prevent such a tragic act. Parents and family are left bereft, inevitably feeling guilty, and full of self-reproach. The interminable 'If only' thoughts are common, but do not help. Parents, family, and friends need professional help to work through these overpowering emotions, and to come to terms with what has happened and their loss. Dr Dinah Jayson says,

> If your son survives a suicide attempt, it is a natural reaction to feel angry. However, try to direct your anger at the behaviour rather than at your child. He will need your understanding, love and support, however upset you may feel. He will also need you to notice if he feels upset or withdrawn, and to listen supportively without judging. If you feel unable to do this, it is better for someone else to take over the support of your child until you feel calmer. Get some support for yourself as well.

■ CASE STUDY – Jonathan's story

Anyone living with a teenager knows that life is often a rollercoaster of emotional highs and lows. Luckily, most teenagers manage to navigate their way through the stormy waters of adolescence without coming to any harm. For others, like Jonathan, life can literally become intolerable.

When seventeen-year-old Jonathan left school last year, it was not to move on to the world of work but to lock himself away in his room. 'He couldn't cope with exams and schoolwork, had no motivation and felt tired all the time,' says his mother, Karen.

At first Karen thought that her son's behaviour might be typical teenage angst, but she soon realized that it was something far more serious. 'He started saying he had let me and everyone down and that he couldn't see any point in living. I suddenly realized that Jonathan was deeply depressed and needed professional help. I had never heard of teenage depression but I got really frightened when he started to talk about the pointlessness of life,' says Karen.

Karen took Jonathan to see her doctor who diagnosed Jonathan's depression. He recommended a course of anti-depressants, which seemed to lift Jonathan's mood for a while. 'But it wasn't until he had professional counselling that he really began to understand the reason for his depression,' states Karen.

The counsellor helped Jonathan to realize that he had never come to terms with the death of his father seven years earlier. 'Because Jonathan was the only male left in the household, he felt a huge burden of responsibility towards me and his sister,' reveals Karen. As well as trying to deal with his grief in private, Jonathan was also under pressure with his GCSEs and was being bullied at school because he no longer had a dad. 'It was just one too many things that tipped him over the edge, and he couldn't see any way out,' says Karen.

Karen was desperately worried that if Jonathan no longer had the motivation to go to school, he would never catch up. However, she talked to the local sixth-form college who have supported Jonathan in retaking his exams, and he has made a fresh start. Karen says:

I would say to any parent who thinks their child may be depressed, try and keep the lines of communication open. Listen when your teenager tells you they can't cope. Encourage them to share their thoughts and feelings with you, and recognize their concerns without judging them. Take it seriously if they say life has no meaning. Tell them that it's not the end of the world if they don't get exams. Face the problem together and do whatever it takes to get them through, even if that means taking them out of school. And never underestimate the pain they are going through. It broke my heart to see Jonathan so low and I honestly don't know what might have happened if we hadn't acted quickly.

8

Different parenting roles

In recent years, attention has focused on the 'breakdown' of the traditional family, and the effect this has on children. It is well known that the extended family of grandparents, aunts and uncles all living in the same cluster of streets is mostly a thing of the past, but there have been even greater changes to the family framework over the last two decades.

> My mum and dad put us first. We always came before their work. I'd rather have had the love than more money.   *Eighteen-year-old*

As you might expect, the majority of children in Great Britain (74 per cent in 2000–2001) grow up in a family with two parents. However, since 1971 when 92 per cent of children lived in a 'couple' family, this percentage has fallen. What is more telling is that the variety of different family structures is increasing. You only have to look at your own circle of friends to see the diversity of family setups and how situations can change – perhaps some friends cohabit, still more are divorced and in a second marriage with a stepfamily, and others have split up and are now heading one-parent families. As a result, today's children are more likely than any other generation to experience a range of different family structures as they grow up.

Before you jump to the conclusion that this can only be a bad thing for kids, recent research is beginning to show that it is the style of parenting rather than the shape of the family that has the greatest influence on our children. The *Leading Lads* report shows that this is particularly true for girls but that 'boys who were not doing so well tended to be strongly associated with low-level fathering whether or not their dad or father figure lived with them'. Doing things together as a family group, from eating meals to having a day out, is very important in the lives of Can-do Boys, the report goes on to explain.

Consequently, if you are a lone parent or head of a stepfamily, you can stop worrying about whether your kids will suffer as a result. A Child Poverty Action Group study showed that despite the worst kinds of poverty, adversity, and bad schooling, some children can and do prosper when they are parented in a supportive style. It is how you parent, rather than your family format that counts. With this important thought in mind, let's take a closer look at some of the various parenting roles and family circumstances, and how these might affect your son.

Mothers and sons
If you are a mother, did you spend nine months speculating about what sex your baby was going to be and yet found yourself faintly surprised when you produced a baby boy? Women seem strangely reluctant to believe that they can nurture and carry something so obviously male inside their female womb.

The Can-do (high self-esteem) Boys in the *Leading Lads* survey talked of parents who:

- Are loving.
- Are very helpful.
- Listen to my problems and views.
- Like me to make my own decisions.
- Get my respect.
- Offer guidance about life.
- Lay down the right rules.
- Treat everyone in the family equally.

What's more, once women have got over the initial shock, they then have to come to terms with the fact that they do not know the first thing about boys. Many mothers feel that they have more of an intuitive understanding of their daughters and that sons are completely alien to them. A mother may not understand what makes her son tick, particularly if she was brought up in a predominantly female household without brothers, for instance.

With a bit of luck, a son is a delightful revelation to a mother – an insight into what it is to be male. On the other hand, he might have been a complete and utter mystery to the mother and she still has not got a clue what is going on inside his head. However, women can always ask a trusted male for some sort of insight if they find themselves bemusedly in the latter category.

As a mother, how you relate to your son depends in some measure on your attitude towards men as a whole and, without dabbling our toes too deeply in the murky waters of psycho-analysis, on your relationship with your father. When reduced to its most simplistic form, it seems that if you've enjoyed a loving relationship with your own father, then you are more likely to be open and affectionate with your son. Your good memories of your father mean that your associations of male-ness are generally positive. Of course, this does not always hold true. Nor does it necessarily mean that if your father was found wanting in the love and affection stakes, that you'll not be able to relate to your son. Yet it has to be acknowledged that your relationship with your father usually has some influence over how you feel about men in general, and your son in particular, even if these feelings are unconscious.

Following this general stream of thought, if you've been on the receiving end of some rough and shabby treatment by men in your adult life, then, on the whole, you're probably not that well disposed towards the male gender. Ipso facto, your views can then colour your attitude towards your 'male' child.

If you come to parenting with a negative view of men, then you have to make extra efforts to help your son feel good about his masculinity, even though it may be hard for you. It is partly up to you to make sure that your son grows up exhibit-ing positive male qualities (rather than just the female virtues you value), and that he does not become the kind of man with whom you've previously had bad experiences.

Whatever your view on men, boys' behaviour can often be puzzling to a mother but you must try to accept your son as he is. That does not mean that you cannot reject certain aspects of his male behaviour, for example, you may ban fighting in your home, but you must still accept your son as a male. So, maybe you can positively help him to find ways to express his aggression through sport, for example, rather than denying or suppressing it completely.

Rejection

It is definitely a learning curve having a son and it helps to keep a curious approach to discovering what it is to be male. View it as a privileged insight into another world, if you like. However, just as you find yourself getting to grips with this alien being and beginning to understand your open and affectionate boy, a complete sea-change in your relationship is about to beset you.

Early adolescence is a particularly difficult time for mothers and their sons. Almost overnight, your cuddly boy becomes aloof and distant. It is as if he cannot bear being near you and you will naturally feel extremely hurt.

The problem is that your son is very uncertain about his awakening sexuality. Adolescent boys are attracted to women and he may become fearful that his strong feelings for you are tainted with some sort of sexual undertones. He does not trust how he feels about women in general, let alone the key woman in his life, namely you, and so he avoids contact until he has worked things out.

This withdrawal can be extremely painful but you have to respect his wishes and keep your distance. Take comfort in the fact that his aloofness does not stem from any sort of dislike of you and that it will change. You'll get your son back once he has a better handle on his sexuality. Sadly, you have to ride the rejection while he attempts to work out what it is to be a man. In the meantime, you have to cover your hurt and help him to feel good about his masculinity – hard though that might be when he is being so mean to you.

What mothers can do
- Keep providing opportunities for conversation.
- Have special one-to-one time doing something practical or active together.
- If he rejects cuddles and kisses, find less obvious ways to show him affection, for example stroking his hair at bedtime or sitting on the settee with him to watch TV – anything that does not make him squirm.
- Continue to bolster his self-esteem.
- Positively reinforce his masculinity when the opportunity arises.

The opposite sex
As an opposite sex parent, you can often play a crucial role in giving your son a rounded view on life. Boys have tender feelings and you can be instrumental in keeping this integral part of your son's character intact. If he is finding it difficult to show affection and love to people, then get him involved in looking after a pet or younger children as an alternative outlet for his emotions.

Mothers are great at teaching boys about life and love. You can help him to relax in female company, tell him about what girls like, and let him know that girls can be mean too. This will all come as a complete eye-opener to him.

The other important role a mother can play is supporting your son in his relationship with his father. You may be better at planning or foreseeing opportunities for the two of them to have some meaningful time together. Maybe you simply need to step back and let your partner be more actively involved in the raising of your son. Often women take the lead in parenting issues and men defer to their partners. It is very easy for strong women to fall into the trap of wanting to provide a bridge between a father and son, where in fact they form a barrier. Sometimes, you have to let a father get on with fathering in his own way, without trying to give too much direction.

There is often a very special and inexplicable bond between a mother and her son. You may find yourself walking a fine line between hating any shows of male arrogance or chauvinism in him, and yet feeling a stab of pain if he is on the receiving end of 'girl power' humiliation. Being female does not prevent you from being close to your son, and it should certainly not prevent you from enjoying his masculinity, despite your desire to also champion women's causes. The aim is to raise sons who will be wonderful partners and great fathers for the next generation.

Fathers and sons

There has been a pendulum swing regarding the role a father plays in child development. If you read parenting books that pre-date the 1960s, you would be forgiven for thinking that once the father has sown his seed, his role is over. However, the pendulum has now swung the other way, with many leading experts, such as Stephen Biddulph and others, stressing the unique and important role that a father has to play in raising his children, especially boys.

> You don't want to let your dad down. You want him to be proud of you.   *Seventeen-year-old*

Certainly, there is much evidence to suggest that boys who grow up with caring, interested, and competent fathers who contribute actively to family life, are more likely to grow up self-confident, and to thrive intellectually and emotionally. There is also evidence that men and women who have had a strong and loving father are more likely to form good relationships, and to have a satisfying marriage.

Mentoring and role models

In traditional societies, the whole male community was involved in preparing a boy for manhood – training, teaching, and initiating him. Today, boys in their mid to late-teens can still benefit from that external male input but our society no longer provides the opportunity. What can individual families do about this?

Short of upping sticks and heading off to Papua New Guinea, the next best thing is to find some trusted men to step in and teach a boy skills, to spend time with him, and to give him a sense of worth beyond his family walls. This role cannot be fulfilled by a father alone – a mentoring role is less nurturing than that of a dad, but it can help to steer a boy on his road towards independence. If you think of the old apprentice system or Fletcher and Godber in *Porridge*, you will get an idea of where we are coming from. The mentoring role can take the heat out of the father-son relationship, particularly at a time when tensions are running high.

However, if you follow this line of argument, the natural conclusion is that if you have an absent father, your prospects are grim. And that is not strictly true. What is important is not that the father is present and plays his part well, but that a family has strong emotional support and input from a man – it can be a grandfather, an uncle or a good family friend. This is a significant fact to hold on to, particularly if you are raising your son as a single mum.

Try to make sure that you have a mixed group of adult friends in which the men are prepared to talk to and invest time in your son. If your partner is sporty and your son is more academic, for example, he's bound to find someone in your circle of friends with whom he can talk, and vice versa of course. Your partner may be an armchair enthusiast, so it may be a family friend who takes the boy out fishing. If a father is willing to allow other good men to have a positive input into his son's life, he will assure his son a more balanced teenage experience.

What many women fail to realize is that men's activities, whether it be fishing, golf, train-spotting or even going to the pub, are not solely about the activity. Just as, if not more, importantly, they provide an opportunity for men to care about each other in an understated way and, in addition, to provide tutelage to young men about what it is to be a man. This is an extraordinarily important function in today's society.

In the UK, men work longer hours than their European counterparts, and many children see their fathers only at breakfast time or at the end of the day. For some, time together is restricted solely to weekends. These excessive working hours and stress are the main reasons why some boys describe their fathers as 'hot emotionally available'.

This 'there, but not there for me' complaint supports the argument that the quality of parenting is more important than a physical presence in the house. A loving father who is separated from his family may be more helpful to his son than a father who is at home but has little time or interest in his kids. A boy may be better off with no dad at all if he has an abusive father.

Nevertheless, it is critical not to underestimate the importance of good male input in your son's life. The *Leading Lads* survey shows that 91 per cent of boys with high self-esteem have highly involved fathers or father figures. This high input father presence also seems to give boys the confidence to show the protective and caring facets of their personalities, to be more optimistic about their life opportunities and prospects, and to take a positive approach to school.

There is also some evidence to suggest that a father can play a key role in his son's ideas about what it is to be a man. If a dad is able to talk openly about his emotions, show his feelings, and also make himself available as a source of emotional support, this highly involved fathering appears to offer some protection against depression or suicidal thoughts in young men.

The only fly in the ointment as far as involved dads are concerned is that in late adolescence, father and son are likely to endure some conflicts. In fact, almost one-third of seventeen- and eighteen-year-old boys say that they get on badly with their father. It is important that a father does not take this 'pulling away' as a personal slight but rather realizes that it is a natural and necessary part of his son's quest for independence. Young men often prefer to take advice and support from another 'important male' instead of their dad at this age and parents can both play a part in providing the right sort of involved men in their son's life. If you are a father, provided that you still make yourself available to your son in every sense, your relationship should survive this temporary cooling off intact.

Divorce and separation

Opinion is polarized on whether or not a couple should stick together in an unhappy relationship for the sake of the kids. You will undoubtedly have your own views based on your friends', family's and, possibly, your own experiences. However, less open to debate is the fact that a family break-up will always cause distress, in varying degrees, to the children involved.

Reactions will always vary depending on the individual child's temperament and the specific circumstances of the break-up, but Judith Wallerstein's study on children of divorced parents in California between 1970 and 1980 has shown that certain patterns of behaviour emerge according to the children's age at the time of the separation. Children below around six years tend to regress and become very clingy. Seven- to eight-year-olds often show signs of depressive symptoms and continue to hope for a reconciliation. This age group can experience real conflicts of loyalty, whereas by the ages of nine to twelve, kids seem to feel the need to take sides. It is interesting that it has always been assumed that older children cope better with a divorce, but research now shows that parental loss can be as traumatic for an adolescent, even one who is almost a young adult and at college. These older adolescents still tend to blame one parent (and rarely blame themselves as younger children do), but many express their anger and hurt by taking the moral high ground.

The bottom line is that there is no good age at which a child's parents can divorce. The separation has to be handled extremely sensitively if the children are not to see the separation as a rejection not just of the other partner, but of them.

What you can do

- *Talk to your children.* Parents can be so preoccupied by their own problems that they do not feel able to talk to their children or they forget to. However, you must make the effort. Your split might have been the result of a long and drawn-out period of conflict but, for the children, it may be sudden and unexpected. Let them know what is happening and why. It is crucial that they are left in no doubt that they are not to blame in any way.
- *Keep older children involved*. Children at secondary school may be mature enough to be involved in decisions that affect their own future, for instance where they want to live. Perhaps what they want is not possible, but at least you have given their wishes some consideration.
- *Try to be civil to each other*. Whatever your feelings, your son needs to feel good about both of you.

If he is blaming one parent and 'siding' with the parent who has been hard done by, the 'wronged' parent should not capitalize on this to get at the other partner.

- **Remember that post-divorce parenting is not a competition.** Resist the temptation to outdo each other with lavish treats and presents in order to become the favourite parent. You are each going to have to evolve your own style of parenting now.
- **Help your son to come to terms with the permanency of the situation.** You do not have to be brutal about it – your son may fantasize about you getting back together because he needs to – but never let him think it is anything more than a remote possibility, not a probability.
- **Consider other family members.** Divorce may mean that your son loses touch with members of the wider family with whom he has been very close. These relatives and friends can supply love and support to your son at a difficult time.
- **Never try to get at each other through your son.** Children cope best if they are allowed and encouraged to maintain good relations with both parents. However, your son may be tempted to play you off against each other and this should not be allowed.
- **Keep things in perspective.** If you are the custodial parent, it may irritate you that your ex-partner, during his or her access weekend, has allowed your son to eat so much ice cream that he is sick, and that he has left his best jacket on the train. But does it really

matter? In the long run, as long as your son is safe, it is not the end of the world if things at the weekend are not conducted as you would have done them. Often, if you are honest, your problem with your ex-partner is not about the food or the jacket but that you have had to relinquish control for a short period and that is what is really irking you.

- ***Try to keep your son's interests at heart.*** Divorce or separation tends to make you focus on your own pain, feelings, and experiences. It takes a constant and conscious effort to keep your son's interests in the forefront of your mind.

What your son wants to know about your divorce

Despite all your concerns, when it boils down to it, there are only a few basic questions that will preoccupy your son:

- Who am I going to live with and do I have a say in it?
- When will I see my mum/dad? Can s/he visit any time or is it only at prearranged times?
- What about my brother(s) and/or sister(s)? Will they be living with me?
- Is it my fault that you split up?
- Does my mum/dad, who is leaving, not love me any more?
- Have you got another man/woman and do I have to meet him/her?
- Will we have to move house?
- Will I have to change schools?
- Is there enough money?

■ PROBLEM SOLVING
Bereavement

Without wishing to sound callous, it is worth knowing that children can suffer more when their parents divorce than they do when they lose a parent through death. Although it is undoubtedly a terrible tragedy and hard for any child to bear, a death is irrevocable and must be accepted. However, a divorce can be revoked and leaves the child with a constant longing for a rapprochement, which also keeps the wound open.

Nonetheless, the loss of a parent is a terrible blow to a child and, at a time when you are reeling with grief, it is not always easy to know how to handle the situation. Here are some ways to make this terrible time of loss more bearable:

- ***Do not be overprotective.*** If your partner or a loved one is dying, it is usually wiser to tell your son. This can help to prepare him for the inevitable and will also prevent him from worrying about what is causing your obvious upset and anxiety (however hard you have tried to hide it).
- ***Encourage him to talk about his feelings.*** He might not respond if you ask him how he is feeling, but if he hears you talking about your own feelings, this may help him to share his grief with you.
- ***Keep him involved.*** It is easy to be so wrapped up in caring for a sick or dying loved one that you leave your son out – let him get involved. Allow him to have a say in the funeral arrangements and to attend. Of course it may be difficult but it will help him to come to terms with what is happening.

- ***Reassure him that you are going to be okay.*** When one parent dies, a child may be better able to cope with the surviving parent's grief if he is reassured that you are going to get through it. He needs to know that he can still turn to you for strength and support even if you are a bit shaky at the moment.

The bereavement charity, Cruse, offers counselling for children as well as for adults, and has a wide range of publications on the topic. Bereavement Line: 0844 477 9400.

Single parents

Whether you are a single parent by choice or as a result of divorce or the death of a partner, you have got your work cut out. It is not that you cannot be a good parent and provide a wonderful family life for your son – of course you can – but you should recognize that it is physically, emotionally, and economically tougher, and these three pressures combined can make life difficult at times.

As a lone parent, you may have to work full-time to support the family, and so you have less time and energy for your son. This in turn can lead to resentment as you see the financial burden coming between you and your family. Equally, your son may resent the fact that he does not have enough of your time, and yet he may also feel guilty because he thinks that you are making sacrifices on his behalf.

Single parents confide that there is almost an intangible pressure for lone parents to prove that they can be successful – either to justify their decision to raise a child alone or to rationalize a divorce. Even though they know this reaction is absolutely unnecessary, they explain that the pressure to prove yourself is almost impossible to resist.

On the plus side, despite all the obstacles, many lone-parent families are extremely close. Your son may feel that he makes a more valuable contribution to family life than his 'couple family' contemporaries, and this gives him self-confidence. You may confide more in each other than many families and deal with problems as a team.

Undoubtedly, if you are a single mum (in nine out of ten cases of separation/divorce, the mother brings up the children and the father lives apart) you can raise your son well, but it is easier if you have the help of a wider network. On your own, the balance between giving love and nurture and maintaining good discipline has to be finely honed, and it is not easy.

Do not allow pride or a misplaced sense of having something to prove condemn you to raising your son in glorious isolation. There is no reason why members of the extended family and friends cannot play a key role in your son's life and, if you are a single mum, some good male influences in your son's life are to be encouraged. For single fathers, the same holds true. Your son needs some positive female influences in his life, although he is more likely to be exposed to female company due to the high number of women in education and child care.

Stepparenting

In the majority of cases, your son does not want a new parent – he simply wants the old one back. Therefore, however happy you might be about a remarriage, do not expect your son to be cock-a-hoop, about the prospect. That said, the results of recent studies may be of some comfort to you. It seems that despite all the possible problems, in most instances a remarriage has no discernible adverse effect on stepchildren's development. This is not to say that there will be no tension, but most enjoy reasonable home relationships. The chances of your son coping well are considerably increased if he can retain contact with both parents – and that holds true whether or not you and your ex-partner are on good terms or not.

If you remarry, your son will have to adapt to two new households, each with a different set of rules and expectations. He may feel that he does not really fit in anywhere and his divided loyalties can make it hard for him to form a close relationship with his new stepparent(s). This can be aggravated still further if stepbrothers and -sisters are involved.

Often a remarriage brings two families together who are out of step with each other. This can mean that you are trying to cope with your own toddlers or maybe a new baby, at the same time as you are trying to establish a relationship with your new adolescent stepson. No wonder it can be stressful.

Many parents who enter into a new relationship are completely oblivious to the fact that children have a magnetic pull on their parents and, as a result, end up feeling jealous of the time their new partner spends with his or her own children.

If you are struggling to cope with the pressures of running a stepfamily or simply feel fed up and in need of a little reassurance, there are numerous mutual support groups aimed at stepparents. These tend to meet once a month and give you an opportunity to meet people in a similar situation, and to discuss issues and coping strategies. However, if you are not a very 'clubbable' person, the National Stepfamily Association helpline may be more useful (tel: 0990 168388).

What you can do
When a stepchild feels rejected and miserable, he or she may become disruptive or even aggressive. To avoid reaching the point where it seems that your stepchild's sole intent is to disrupt your marriage, here are some guidelines:

- ***Before you remarry, give all the children involved plenty of warning.*** Encourage them to speak about their fears and feelings, and explain how you are feeling.
- ***Do not exclude the natural parent.*** Be kind and helpful to your new stepchildren, but never try to replace the real parent. Children will adapt more readily to a new stepfamily if they do not feel their absent parent is being superseded and if they can see him/her regularly.
- ***Do not rush in.*** If two families are to merge, the children need time to get to know each other before they start sharing a home.
- ***Discuss changes in lifestyle.*** If your remarriage results in major disruption in your son's life, such as having to share a room, move house or change schools, it is important to acknowledge that these are potential problems, to discuss them, and to try to solve them.
- ***Ground rules.*** If stepsiblings are involved, accept that new ground rules will have to be worked out and that there may be difficulties until each set of kids gets used to doing things a different way.
- ***Join a mutual support group for your children.*** Even if it is not your cup of tea, the support given to

children in reordered families is woefully inadequate, particularly if they seem to be coping well. The children who 'create' may get some attention, but those who keep their feelings under wraps 'because they don't want to let you down' get precious little help, when in fact they may be feeling wretched inside.

- *Do not neglect your new marriage.* Although it is important to give time and consideration to the children, this should not be at the cost of the relationship. After all, it is in their best interest for your marriage to be successful (although they may not see it that way at the time).

■ PROBLEM SOLVING
My son has run away from home
Every year, about 45,000 young people run away from home. Most are between fourteen to sixteen years old and the numbers are fairly equally split between boys and girls. If your son runs away from home, there is a very good chance that you will know the reason why. However, in some cases, his disappearance can be the first indication that something is amiss. The three main reasons cited by young people for running away are:

1. *Frequent family rows, usually about the youngster's behaviour.* If your son feels that you are not really listening to him or that you do not understand how he feels, he may decide that running away is the only way to make you see how strongly he feels.
2. *He is worried about a problem that he is afraid to talk to you about.* If your son feels that you might

react angrily or be hurt if he tells you about a certain problem, running away may seem like the easiest way out of his dilemma. Bullying, exam stress, getting a girl pregnant or concerns about his sexual orientation are all problems that he might dread telling you about. Rather than face the music, your son might run away before you hear about an impending suspension from school, a brush with the law or an alcohol, drug or debt problem.

3. ***Something at home is making his life unbearable.*** Hard though it is to accept, sometimes it is a situation at home that seems inescapable and insoluble to your son that causes him to run away. Maybe he cannot get on with a stepparent or, more seriously, perhaps he is being physically, emotionally or sexually abused. These are not problems that your son can resolve within the family and he may feel his only recourse is flight. These are the sort of problems that are also hardest for a parent to face but, before your son can come home safely, these issues have to be addressed.

What you can do
If your son runs away:

- ***Check with the parents of his friends.*** This is your first port of call because many young runaways go to a best friend's house. In fact, 98 per cent stay in their own area, mostly with friends or relatives.
- ***Check with relatives.*** Particularly if he is close to a specific grandparent or uncle, for instance.

- ***If you still do not know his whereabouts.*** Contact the local police.
- ***Try to stay calm.*** Nigh on impossible, but try to keep in mind that most children who run away are home within forty-eight hours.
- ***When he does come home.*** You are likely to weep with relief and then explode with anger. Whatever your reaction, make it clear that it is because you love him and were so worried about him.
- ***Do not forget the original problem.*** After the general jubilation at his return, it is easy to lose sight of the fact that he left because there was a problem. Make it clear to him that you want to understand why he felt he had to run away. Listen attentively and without butting in, and then discuss with him what you can do to sort things out.
- ***It may be a problem that needs outside help.*** Your son may want to talk to someone who is not directly involved. Professional counselling may help.

■ CASE STUDY – Jan's story

Having teenage stepchildren and a young family of your own can put you under considerable strain, as Jan discovered.

'I was twenty-three when I first met Martin's boys. Stuart was twelve and James nine. Initially it was fine – their mother had a boyfriend and was happy, and the boys seemed happy to spend time with both their mother and their father with their respective new "partners".

'I was particularly "cool" as I was young, drove a sports car, sunbathed topless and would answer questions about orgasms and sex generally, which they didn't feel happy asking their parents. They were bewildered that I shared a bedroom with their father, but it wasn't a major issue.

'Within the first twelve months a holiday was booked with their dad and he wanted to take me too. Their mum was not impressed and said I was too young to cope with the boys and would distract Martin from them. In hindsight she was right. At the time, Martin was very upset and said that he would not go without me, and so she would not let the boys come. It was a few years later that James commented to me "we couldn't go on that holiday because you were there" but Martin intervened with "you did not come on that holiday because your mother wouldn't let you".

'Time passed – their mother left her partner and then made advances to Martin in an attempt to win him back. I don't think my presence affected his decision not to rekindle their relationship – he had realized how unhappy their marriage had been once he was on his own. But this was a major turning point. She became very bitter and from that day to this (nineteen years) has blamed me for the breakdown of their marriage.

'James was eleven years old by this time. Stuart was about fourteen and looking more and more like his father every day – he was not his mother's favourite child. I was two years older too and starting to resent their presence. The novelty was wearing off. I was still too young to understand what the boys needed. On some weekends I would not be around for their visit and though the boys enjoyed having Martin to themselves, particularly James, Martin was not happy having them without me being around. I should have realized that despite what Martin wanted, Stuart and James really needed him alone – their mother tried to make this point but her manner with dealing with us as a couple was not conducive to a positive response!

'James and I really did not enjoy being together – we did not like each other. Stuart and I share similar star signs and therefore understood each other well; we had some happy times together. James resented my presence: if I asked him to put something away in our house he would insist that it was nothing to do with me, and would only do something if their dad asked. Holidays with the boys were allowed by their mother, but painful. James and I did not want to be together. I made attempts to be friends with him but was constantly rebuffed or ignored.

'Four years later, when the boys found out I was pregnant, Stuart was delighted – James was sure he would not be related and therefore disinterested. When it was explained to him that their dad was a common bond, he showed some interest, and even came with me for my scan. When our daughter was born James was besotted, but I was still persona non grata.

'About this time, Stuart came to live with us, he was eighteen. It was wonderful. James and I became more distant – he wouldn't come to the house and would only see Martin alone and on neutral territory. This was fine with me, I was a new mum and didn't want a sulky teenager around. Time passed and I felt that our daughter missed out – she had one half-brother living with her and another who she never saw.

'James started causing problems for his mother, drinking, taking drugs, and then failing A levels. Stuart moved out and went to university, and James came to live with us – he wanted to! He was very difficult to live with – he was almost always high on drugs or drunk. He got himself a job at the local pub and got in with some local hoodlums. Eventually Martin took things in hand and booked James in for psychiatric help. James's drinking problem is hereditary and Martin took him to the same psychiatrist who had helped him. James offloaded his understanding of the breakdown of his parents' marriage, which amazed Martin. The story that James had was a long way from the truth, but one that his mother had instilled in him. It was too far in his subconscious for anyone to be able to unravel. I was never invited to these sessions, but it came out how much James disliked me.

'Every time after a session James would come home and say "hello" but that would be it. I was amazed when Martin told me what had been said. I asked to be involved but was discouraged – James didn't want it.

'Once we were talking about divorce and children and James said, "We are the innocent victims – it's not our fault we get angry – we have no say in the matter."

'I became pregnant again and James was appalled – he couldn't understand why we hadn't involved him in our decision. "Why do you keep having these people that are going to be related to me but you do not ask me first?'

'Eventually James left our home. What a relief. He had hardly spoken to me; one time we asked him to be home to babysit and he had purposely not turned up. We gave him a lot of rope to hang himself and he just kept on unravelling it. Many, many times I thought about leaving but felt it unreasonable to ask Martin to choose. Everyone said things would get better.

'James and I didn't really see each other for a few years once he'd moved out – Martin would see him alone or with our two children.

'In the last three years James has had a girlfriend (who is now his wife). He is twenty-seven years old. Things have got better but not before he found a girl he was serious about. It is almost as though he had to fall in love to understand Martin's and my relationship, and also as he has got older he has understood how his mother's mind works. She is extremely manipulative, still bitter, and still alone. It takes a grown man to realize how she operates.

'We have talked about his drinking problem but never about our problem with each other. I would like to think we can talk about it but then I think maybe we should just move on.

'We have never said sorry. I was the adult and should have understood the situation better. I have a son now and can see what the relationship is between a mother and son. I couldn't have known this before, I was too young.

'I wasn't trying to take his mother's place – something I think she always feared. My relationship with James has not been helped by his parents' continual dislike for each other and his mother's anger at my presence.

'James is very good with our two children (twelve and nine) and frequently babysits for us now. Each year gets better – maybe one day I can sit down and apologize for all the hurt that has happened – maybe I should just move on.'

9

School's out …
Boys in education

The fact that you are reading this book suggests that you are a caring, proactive parent who most likely offers your son support and encouragement with his education, and works in partnership with his teachers and school. You are probably happy that your son will achieve good, or at least acceptable, academic results, and that he will go on to pursue the career or further education he desires. Perhaps you are not greatly alarmed by the blaring headlines about girls outstripping boys in almost every subject area because it does not directly affect your family.

However, indirectly, the general movement towards boys' disaffection from learning, the lack of male role models in education, bullying, and increasing discipline problems can and will impinge on your son's attitude to learning, and could dictate whether or not he enjoys his school days and achieves his potential.

Currently schools are not catering for boys' needs. Teachers are struggling to cope with increased paperwork and national targets and, with the best will in the world, the net result is that instead of teaching creatively and with enthusiasm, they often end up putting what little time and energy they have left into making sure that girls achieve and boys behave.

It's all in your head

It is now known that a baby boy's brain develops more slowly than a baby girl's, which is one of the reasons that some experts recommend that boys start their primary education a year after girls.

In addition, the left and right sides of a boy's brain form fewer connections, although his brain is richer in internal connections on the right side – a possible explanation for boys' greater success in mathematics and mechanics, which are governed by this side of the brain.

The left hemisphere of the brain handles language and reasoning, and the right governs movement, emotion, and spatial awareness. Studies using brain-scanning technology by Bennett and Shaywitz' 'Sex Differences in the Functional Organization of the Brain for Language' published in *Nature* in 1995 show that boys may use only one side of their brain to tackle certain kinds of problems, such as spelling tests and language games, whereas girls use both sides, which gives them the edge.

One of the disadvantages of a less connected right and left hemisphere can be that a boy has greater

The conscious decision in the 1980s to increase emphasis on verbal skills (which generally favours girls) and to reduce competitive testing (which previously tended to favour boys) has contributed to girls' academic achievements surpassing

difficulty in skills that involve both sides of the brain, such as reading or talking about feelings.

However, the right side of the brain also governs feelings – so never doubt that your son is experiencing emotions, but it takes him extra effort to shift into his left hemisphere to express the emotions that he is registering in his right hemisphere.

Understanding the influences of different brain development can help parents to reconcile why boys may face certain practical difficulties in education.

It is also useful to bear in mind when you feel the temptation to draw direct parallels between your son and his sister or female counterparts. Remember that boys are not inferior to girls, they simply develop differently.

Schools have long had programmes to help girls in mathematics and sciences, and only now are we starting to see boys being encouraged in English, Drama, and so forth. If you can add language and expressive skills to his already impressive arsenal of thinking and action skills, consider what a well-rounded, fabulous adult your son could be.

boys'. Boys perform considerably less well than girls in GCSE examinations and girls have been making greater progress between the ages of eleven and sixteen too. Key Stage tests show that girls get off to a better start in reading than boys but, more surprisingly, the lead continues through Key Stages 2 and 3.

Unfortunately, rather than rising to the challenge, boys seem to have responded to girls' superior academic achievements by becoming less motivated, messing around rather than facing failure or peer group scorn, and even opting out of education altogether. It seems that in education, girls compete and boys retreat.

This trend has concerned educationalists and parents for some time now, and a growing number of schools are introducing and reintroducing ways in which boys may be encouraged to achieve their full potential. It is widely acknowledged that boys need additional help and encouragement to master written language, to enjoy reading, and to express themselves verbally.

A few secondary schools are addressing the issue of boys and girls developing differently by separating boys from girls for English classes. In this way, the choice of materials can be tailored specifically to boys' or girls' tastes, and the boys can enjoy some intensive literacy support. Although this solution is not without risks (for example, the gender stereotype trap of war poems for boys and love poems for girls), so far, the results have been impressive. It is thought that boys are more likely to speak up if they are not frightened of looking stupid in front of the more articulate girls. It then follows that if boys do not have to mess around to cover their inadequacies, they begin to experiment more with reading, acting, and poetry, etc. This has helped with their acquisition of the language skills that are so essential for effective communication and self-expression in every aspect of adult life.

Nonetheless, as parents, you probably recognize that for most boys, the quiet, compliant, passive approach to learning that is fostered in the vast majority of schools is a complete contrast, even anathema, to your son's naturally exuberant, energetic, and physically active approach to life. In good schools, this passion and vitality is harnessed and directed into boys' learning, and allowances are made for the fact that boys and girls tend to learn differently. However, when boys' vitality is quashed or ignored, because it is easier to watch over a classroom full of children sitting quietly at desks than to have bodies flying around, this energy can be misdirected into misbehaviour and disruption.

Although this may sound bleak, let's not get too carried away with statistics. There are plenty of boys who still enjoy going to school each day, and who perform very well despite all of the obstacles. Yet simply knowing that, for some, school is a battlefield where boys walk a fine line between credibility among their peers or derision, and achieving academically or not, it is easier for parents to understand and support them in the problems that they may face on a daily basis.

However, recognizing and catering for boys' needs does not have to be at the expense of girls' learning and achievements. Despite the media's taste for sensationalism, there is no need to turn education into a girls-versus-boys debate. Schools should quite rightly celebrate and encourage girls' recent successes, and at the same time you have a right to

> I've experienced exam stress but not to the extent of it affecting my health. It builds up and that's why I'm taking a gap year.   *Seventeen-year-old*

expect them to look at ways to make sure that boys also perform well in the classroom.

During interviews, parents repeatedly cited various aspects of boys in education as causes for concern. Here follows some feedback from the discussions and the advice received from parents and experts alike.

Exam stress

It is only natural for your son to have some anxiety about tests and exams. In fact, it is probably more useful than a cavalier or blasé attitude. Nevertheless, when exam nerves become so crippling that he cannot concentrate and makes mistakes, this is when stress becomes distress, and something needs to be done.

In the *Leading Lads* survey findings, schoolwork and exams was the number one cause of stress for both Can-do and Low Can-do Boys, particularly among those with high self-esteem (69 per cent).

Does your son complain of any of the following exam stress symptoms?

- Racing heart.
- Erratic breathing.
- Feeling extremely hot or cold in the exam room.
- Tension headache.
- Upset stomach.

> My parents appreciated exam stress. They have a
> tacit understanding and agreement – they cut me
> more slack.   *Nineteen-year-old*

- Frequent trips to the toilet.
- Muddled thinking.
- Distracted by environment and circumstances.

If he does, you might like to think about taking some active steps to help him.

What you can do
- He needs as much practice as possible at previous papers and 'mocks'. Then he can evaluate whether his revision techniques and the way he approached the paper are working or not.
- Reiterate what the teacher will undoubtedly have told him about exam technique: check the number of questions in total; read the questions carefully; allow plenty of time; do not panic and do not rush in. All sound advice but, in reality, it may fly out of the window under pressure, so be tolerant if he messes up.
- Provide plenty of information. It has been shown that children are less anxious about tests when they know the facts, i.e. what the test is designed to discover, how long it will take and how it will be marked.
- Encourage him to use a relaxation technique, such as yoga or meditation. He could attend classes so

> You don't admit that you're under stress at fourteen but at seventeen you might. People acknowledge a lot more about how much work you've been doing and how much stress you're experiencing.
>
> *Eighteen-year-old*

that the technique can be mastered long before exam time.

- If he balks at the idea of relaxation techniques and dismisses them as something for old hippies, then get him to practise the following routine to calm down: breathe in to a count of four, hold for a count of four, and then slowly breathe out to a count of eight. Visualizing blue on the in-breath and gold on the out-breath is especially beneficial, if he will do it. A more physical technique is to start from the toes and work up through the body, tensing and relaxing muscles as he goes.

■ PROBLEM SOLVING

The school plan to suspend my son

In 2001, more than 9,000 pupils were removed from schools in England for violent and disruptive behaviour, and bullying or drug-related incidents, up from just over 8,000 the previous year.

If your son has been heading for this kind of trouble, you should have been consulted by the school long before you get to the stage of exclusion, and every effort should have been made by you and the school to avert such a drastic measure. As former UK Education Secretary Estelle Morris says, 'Exclusion is a last resort and is only used with good reason.

Our [the UK Government's] priority is to support head teachers who take tough decisions when dealing with bad or criminal behaviour.'

Exclusion can last for a fixed period of days, for an indefinite period or, in very rare and extreme cases, permanently. In any event, you should be informed of the reasons for the exclusion order and its duration. You then have the right to appeal, usually to either the school governors or the local education authority. In fact, in 2001, parental appeals against their children's exclusion were up 15 per cent on the previous year, at 1,095. However, independent appeals panels returned fewer pupils to school, with verdicts in parents' favour down by 5 per cent to just under 32 per cent.

Before you appeal:
- Make sure of your facts and the events leading up to the exclusion.
- Check out your son's school record to make sure that it is consistent with the reasons for his exclusion.
- Did the school make all reasonable efforts to deal with trouble appropriately before this step?
- Ask why the school has resorted to such a severe punishment, particularly if it is a first offence.
- Speak to teaching staff and classroom assistants to see if his behaviour was exceptional or if he is being singled out.
- Keep copies of all correspondence and notes from any meetings leading up to your appeal.
- Encourage your son to attend the meeting also and, if you don't have a partner to go with you, get a friend or member of the family to attend so that s/he can take notes.

- Difficult though it may be, try to be objective and stay calm. If you are to put a persuasive case, it does not help to be emotional or abusive.
- Attempt to stay on good terms with teaching staff since, if your appeal is successful, your son will stay at the school and you (and he) will have to deal with them.

Boys and sport

In the main, sports can be a great asset to boys, but it is something of a double-edged sword, and not only for the non-athletic. Even for those boys with natural ability, if exposed to the wrong kind of 'jock' culture, sport can be damaging.

Nonetheless, the overall benefits of sport in school for boys are indisputable. Team sports can give a boy a sense of belonging, can build character, and boost self-esteem, not to mention the health benefits. It can provide a great opportunity for boys to be more open and to show affection to each other – offering praise for good efforts and comfort for that missed opportunity, exchanging hints and tips, and sharing humour and warmth through team camaraderie.

As a male bonding exercise sport, either in or out of school, can offer a boy a chance to become closer to his father. Watching a match together or supporting his son from the touchline can be a bonding and uplifting experience for both.

For many boys, a love of sport (irrespective of their ability) is a unifying force. Perhaps it allows them entry into the in-crowd or, more commonly, it is the opening gambit that allows boys to strike up conversation with other kids that they do not know. Those who do not play well might develop a staggering knowledge of the football league, for example, reeling off players and results with ease. This too confers credibility and an acceptance by peers.

With the right approach and good coaching, sport can teach boys:

- How to win and lose with good grace.
- How to be a team player (i.e. cooperation, support of others, recognizing strengths and weaknesses).
- How to persevere even when you are tired or being beaten.
- How practice makes perfect (or better anyway).
- How to work towards an objective, for example the junior league trophy.

All of these skills will equip him well for adulthood. Yet despite these benefits, which should turn your son into a better person, there can be a flip side to childhood sport. Sport conveys a powerful message, especially to boys and, if not handled correctly, all sorts of unwholesome ideas can be picked up. Nowhere are you more likely to come across displays of bad language, violence, bad temper, egotism, sexism, homophobia or racism than on a sports field. That is why coaches, teachers, trainers, parents, and officials alike have a responsibility to instil in players notions of being good sports, and to clamp down immediately on demonstrations of sporting machismo.

Of course, by its very nature, sport encourages competitiveness which, whether you like it or not, appeals to most boys. Unfortunately, for every winner there is one or

> At fourteen, it matters if you're no good at sport. I hung
> out with the anti-jocks but it was difficult.
>
> *Eighteen-year-old*

more losers. With correct handling, many argue that this is an important lesson to learn from a young age. However, a more insidious side to competitive sport is when your son is the one who is always picked last for the team. Since sport is one of the few arenas in which the peer group allows a boy to build a positive image of himself, for the boy who feels he is a sporting failure, this can badly affect his self-esteem.

If a boy shows great sporting talent, it is important that parents guard against the temptation for the school and involved adults to use his sporting success for their own gratification. It is always inviting to bathe in reflected glory, but this can put undue pressure on a boy to perform well and achieve greatness. This in turn can lead to overtraining or, worse, use of drugs to maintain or improve performance.

The final and probably most common problem of boys in sport is when parental expectation rears its ugly head. Although we have seen that sport can bring parents and sons together – sometimes it is the only thing that grown men and their fathers can talk about – when a parent is frustrated by their son's lack of sporting prowess and shows it, untold damage can be done to their relationship. Many previously sporty parents are aware of the dangers of putting undue pressure on their non-athletic sons, but seem powerless to do anything about or to hide their disappointment. A confident parent should be just as proud if his son shows

> It's an advantage if you're sporty but not insurmount-
> able if not.   *Fifteen-year-old*

ability in other areas, but it does not always work that way. Equally, a parent, particularly a father, who is not physical or is disinterested in sport can be an embarrassment for a boy who loves it. Basically, sport can be a minefield if not approached sensitively.

Gifted children

There is no particular definition of the term 'gifted', but those who have researched the topic agree that children with exceptional abilities can be roughly divided into two groups.

Usually, when you think of a gifted child, you call to mind a child prodigy, such as Mozart. However, there is a second group of gifted children that comprises the exceptionally talented all-rounder. This child is very good at whatever he turns his hand to, from sport to academic achievements. Such a gift is a great advantage and a child with this particular sort of talent tends to do exceptionally well. Since such children are not spectacularly clever or talented in any one particular field, they can still mix well with their classmates, and they are usually sociable, well-adjusted children.

Yet the commonly accepted image of the gifted child is the headline-grabbing prodigy who excels in one particular area. This may be in the form of an exceptional intelligence, or an outstanding talent for music, maths, sport, chess or whatever. Although gifted children in total make up about 10 per cent of the population, these child prodigies are very rare and, because they are so obviously different from their peers, they may have problems fitting in.

Realistically, raising a gifted child can demand additional effort and, in some cases, sacrifice from parents. A son with a prodigious talent will need plenty of opportunity to practise those skills, and you have to commit yourself to spending many hours (and sometimes a great deal of money) on watching practice sessions and ferrying him to and from lessons, workouts, etc.

This degree of parental support may, at first sight, seem like the least you can do. After all, don't you have an obligation to help your child fulfil his potential? However, when there are other children in the family, such a commitment is less straightforward. Just because one child has a talent, it does not automatically mean that he has priority rights to his parents' time and resources. If you have to spend an inordinate amount of time, energy, and money on your gifted child, there is a good chance that his siblings will experience varying degrees of rejection and resentment. How you balance the amount you invest in each family member has to be finely judged.

If your child is intellectually gifted, you may find that his mainstream schoolwork is not challenging enough for him. Involve the school and his teachers in discussions about his abilities, and how to maximize these within the framework of the curriculum. An assessment from an educational psychologist may help the child's teacher to devise a specially tailored work programme and to build in appropriate stimulus.

When a child is musically or athletically gifted, he needs specialist tuition, which will need to be continually reassessed and upgraded as his talent develops. In some instances, specialist schools, such as a music academy, might be an option.

The non-academic child

It's not always easy to assess what your son is capable of. A natural tendency for parents to over-egg their children's abilities, coupled with boys' natural tendency to do as little work as it is possible to get away with, can lead to a discrepancy in expectations and achievements.

Nonetheless, it has to be accepted that not all children are academic high achievers and this may be difficult to accept if the rest of the family, and you as parents, are high-flyers.

If you and the school agree that your son is not academically inclined, try to accept this and work on ways for him to get the most out of his education programme. Children who feel that they should be able to do well in class but are failing can become bewildered and depressed. Behaviour may deteriorate if he cannot, rather than will not, do what is expected of him in school.

If you cannot decide whether you are expecting too much of your son or if there is another reason for his lack of results, you could consult an educational psychologist for specialized testing. However, although some parents refuse to believe there is not some specific cause which limits their son's achievements, in the main, caring parents recognize in their heart of hearts when their son is non-academic, and concentrate on his other strengths.

However much time and effort you devote to your child's talent, it should always be borne in mind that this is only one small aspect of his development. He still needs the same love, freedom, and direction as any other child. Accept that he has a great gift but recognize that this is only one part of what makes him who he is, and love him warts and all.

What you can do
Preventing burnout:

- Encourage your child, but do not put him under pressure to achieve.
- Do not make him feel obliged to do well because of what you have done for him.
- Enlist the support of the school and teachers so that they understand that your child has 'special needs', if not in the accepted sense.
- Network through organizations such as the Association of Gifted Children. Meet with parents of other gifted children who understand the pressures and stresses of being and having a gifted child.
- While concentrating on his talent, try to keep his interests broad and then if it all goes horribly wrong, he still has a life outside his gift. Who knows, he may have other potential areas of expertise?

Keeping his interest:
- Your child may not enjoy what you enjoy. Just because you can see enormous potential in one area, encourage broad interests, and let him choose his favoured option. If you have pushed him into something, no matter how

great his talent, he will never excel because the desire is not there and he will get out as soon as possible.

- Help him to understand that he can try something new, but that he has to give it a chance. Agree to stick with it for a few months before deciding whether or not to continue.
- Do not put the emphasis on success all the time because failure is occasionally inevitable. If your child thinks he has disappointed you, it may demotivate him.
- Be supportive without being domineering.
- Make practice fun. To be a prodigy, he will need lots of practice so keep it informal and laid back rather than a chore. If it is fun, he will get into the habit of practising and stick with it.
- Give him some space. However gifted, he still needs time to discover who he is and to relax like the rest of us.

Dropping off in schoolwork

In adolescence, many boys go through a period where their schoolwork suffers, usually temporarily. There can be many causes for this – health problems, relationships with girls, mood swings, exam stress – whatever the reason, it is important that you get him to talk about it. If he plays down the problem with you, see if you can persuade a trusted teacher or family friend to have an informal chat with him.

What you can do

Here are some tips for keeping him on an even keel at school:

- Watch out for problems with hearing loss or eyesight, which are common causes of decline in schoolwork in adolescence.

- It can be hard for teenagers to balance social life and school – either too much time spent on fun, friends and the phone or too many hours slogging away at homework. Help him to get the balance right by himself or by imposing rules if necessary.
- Encourage him to talk about any causes for anxiety before they become problems.
- If he is struggling in one particular school subject, an outside tutor may be all that is needed to restore confidence and improve performance.
- If exam stress is the root cause, help him with exam and relaxation techniques.

Hothousing

There is a recognized syndrome that occurs around the age of thirteen in children who have been tutored and pressurized for years – they peak. They have been working flat out for so long that they simply cannot keep it up.

If a child has been hothoused to get into a certain school or to achieve some adult-ordained peak of performance, his accomplishments are not a true reflection of his ability but rather of the incredible input he has received. The problem is that with or without this level of input, he simply cannot continue to grow at the same rate.

Our society seems obsessed with speeding up development and achievement – how could any parent fail to sign up his beloved son for baby gymnastics and preschool French lessons? Yet educationalists and

Boys' disaffection with learning

'School is a waste of time' is the conclusion that an increasing number of boys have drawn by the time they reach secondary school. This statement is echoed by the statistics that show that boys are underachieving, even in traditionally male subjects.

It is now known that boys at the age of six or seven (when they have been in school a couple of years) are on average six to twelve months less well developed mentally than girls. The delay is particularly marked in the area of their fine motor skills which, to you and me, is holding a pencil, using scissors, etc. They are also still in the stage of 'gross motor' development,

psychologists agree that hothousing, where a child is pushed from task to task to improve performance, is damaging in the extreme, and likely to backfire. Remember:

- Pushing a child too hard undermines his confidence and ensures failure.
- If he is always being pushed on to the next goal, he does not have time to feel good about what he has achieved.
- Children who are pushed may not be able to learn without external pressure. It is important for later success that a child establishes his own motivation.
- Children need sufficient free time to potter around and to learn that it is fine to be relaxed and quiet sometimes.
- If you force your son now he may reject the subject later.

which means that it is physically hard for them to sit still for any length of time.

Stressed primary teachers often tell boys off for what appears to be misbehaviour, such as fidgeting and leaping about. If, through a boy's eyes, you combine this 'injustice' with seeing his female classmates drawing, writing, and reading better than him, then it is not surprising that boys start to switch off from learning, even at this early age.

Sadly, when boys' desire for action is met with reprimands, they form even stronger anti-learning attitudes. Some even revel in the spotlight of being 'the bad boy of the class', since they believe this enhances their macho status.

If you look at these stark realities for boys in education, you can see why girls generally have an early advantage:

- Boys often bridle at fitting into a classroom culture that rewards quiet, fine motor, indoor, verbal, and written kinds of activity.
- Very few schools use teaching methods that encourage rather than repress masculine qualities.
- As a general rule verbal skills are considered of greater importance in the educational system than spatial skills.
- The majority of teachers in primary schools are women and learning becomes a 'female' or 'non-male' activity.
- A boy's need to assert himself often takes the form of being noisy or jokey in the classroom.
- Boys do not like to risk failure or to lose face and many opt out of learning challenges where they might not succeed.

- As risk-takers, many boys prefer to be involved in action rather than the confining nature of reading and writing at a desk.
- If boys are labelled as difficult in the classroom, they will live up to expectations.
- Changes in the job market mean that boys can no longer be sure of a permanent job at the end of their schooling, which can also dissuade boys from applying themselves to schoolwork.

Without wishing to turn back the clock so that girls are again disadvantaged, what can parents and schools do to boost boys' learning?

In fact, schools in the UK have already started. Several initiatives are being implemented, ranging from trying to attract more men into teaching at primary schools to reintroducing competitive testing, and segregating the sexes at GCSE for certain subjects. There is a growing awareness in schools of the difficulties faced by boys and a desire to develop strategies to help them. However, what about the parents' role?

What you can do

- Maintain a boy's interest in reading books by making sure that they read with their father or other important males. Also, choose subject matter carefully to appeal, bearing in mind that boys often prefer non-fiction.
- Help your son to be more articulate by encouraging discussion in your home.
- Supervise homework to make sure he does it to the best of his ability, and to promote pride in his work.

> People get bullied because they are complete los-
> ers. Sometimes it's attention-seeking – they're almost
> asking for it.   *Fourteen-year-old*

- Recognize boys' natural need to blast off excess energy by keeping homework to short, intensive bursts.
- Build physical activity into his daily life wherever possible.

Bullying

In a Childline study into bullying in schools, 64 per cent of primary school children said they had been bullied at some point at school. Ninety-four per cent of children said they had experienced verbal abuse, 56 per cent physical abuse and 51 per cent both.

For many, personal safety, both emotional and physical, cannot be guaranteed, and boys in particular view school as a jungle.

However, the school has a responsibility to stop bullying and most now implement a whole school 'anti-bullying' policy with procedures that are clearly established to deal with any incidents.

Persistent bullying can have a devastating effect on your son's self-esteem. He may feel that it is somehow his fault or that there is something wrong with him. Bullying can make a boy more withdrawn, insecure, and cautious. Days and sometimes years of victimization can lead many youngsters to depression and others to suicide.

You accept bullying and teasing as part of growing up. If you are always Mr Popular, you will grow up ill-prepared for life. *Eighteen-year-old*

Even if you enjoy a good relationship with your son, this is no guarantee that he will tell you if he is being bullied. Around 50 per cent of children who are bullied at school do not report their experiences, often because they are afraid of greater intimidation from their tormentors. Signs you can look out for include:

- A reluctance to go to school or a change in routine such as a different route or asking to be driven.
- Physical signs such as bruises, scratches or damage to clothing and possessions.
- Dropping off in schoolwork.
- Frequent 'loss' of dinner money with inadequate explanations of how it has been spent.
- A lack of friends and invitations to play/parties.

What you can do
If you suspect bullying, you should act. Ask him if he is being bullied or threatened, and explain that you are concerned for his well-being. If he does not confess straight away, make it clear that you are there for him at any time. If he does admit to being bullied, your first step should be to reassure your child, to praise him for telling you, and to assure him of your support. Then things become a little more complicated.

It is a natural reaction to try to impose a solution to protect your child, but you must also consult his wishes or he may feel

> In a big school, it's easy to get caught up in the bully-
> ing culture.   *Sixteen-year-old*

even more powerless and vulnerable. Here are some suggestions you can discuss with your son:

- Recommend that he tells a teacher that he likes and
  trusts about the problem or offer to contact the school
  yourself.
- If you are not satisfied with the school's response, talk
  to a parent governor about the problem. Do not let
  them treat this lightly (see Jan and Paul's Story, page
  208) – if necessary contact your MP.
- Point out that retaliating with physical violence
  (as often advocated by grandparents) can make
  matters worse, could get your son seriously hurt,
  and might even turn the bullied into a bully. On the
  other hand, if you expressly forbid him to use force
  under any circumstances, he may feel exposed
  and vulnerable. It is a difficult call but make sure
  he understands that self-defence is only used as
  a last resort.
- Explain that your son has a right to keep himself safe.
  Allow him to use whatever works for him – running
  away, using assertiveness skills, telling an adult, strik-
  ing back.
- Point out that friends are the best protection against
  bullying. Just one good friend can make the difference. Let him know that friends are welcome at
  home.

> It's very rare for someone to stand up and try to stick up for someone who's being bullied. It's dealt with in a more subtle way.　　　　　　*Eighteen-year-old*

- Help him to work out how to avoid places and situations which are conducive to bullies.
- Explain that buying off a bully does not work in the long term and he should not give in to demands for money.
- Invest in your son's resilience. Research shows that having good social and communication skills and self-esteem diminishes the likelihood of being bullied.

Bullying can take a long time to resolve and the psychological scars from bullying may last even longer. Your child will need a lot of emotional support, and groups and charities such as Kidscape, the NSPCC or ChildLine (see pages 311-314) can offer help and advice.

■ PROBLEM SOLVING
My son is bullying other kids

For any parent, it is a devastating blow to be told that your son is guilty of bullying. While in no way wishing to undermine the horror or the severity of the situation if your child is a victim of bullying, it is true to say that people's reaction are usually of sympathy and help. If your son is a bully, he and you may be regarded with distaste and revulsion.

Your first reaction is probably one of disbelief or even anger but, if you are presented with facts, you must accept it and look for a reason why your son is behaving in this way.

Has something happened that could trigger such a change in character? Are new siblings or stepsiblings causing tension and jealousy? Are you or your partner away from home more? Are there domestic tensions, rows, a separation or divorce?

Bullies often feel inadequate or unloved or may themselves be the victim of harsh regimes at home. Others are simply caught up by the crowd and do not want to draw fire by speaking out. Some are simply used to always getting what they want and cannot negotiate or compromise. Although there may be reasons, there can be no justification for bullying and you must act quickly and decisively.

What you can do
It is hard to accept that your child is in the wrong, but he needs your help to change his behaviour, and there is no time to lose because another child's life is being made miserable.

- Do not overreact by shouting and haranguing your son. Calmly tell him that although you love him, you do not like his behaviour.
- Talk about the behaviour rather than labelling him a bully.
- Explain what bullying behaviour is and why it can be hurtful and damaging.
- Give him help to develop skills to negotiate conflict, and to communicate and manage his emotions.
- Ask him how he thinks he could stop bullying. Help him to feel part of the solution, not simply 'the problem'.
- Recognize that this will not happen overnight. Encourage him when he reduces bullying behaviour.

- An apology to the victim in writing or verbally may help, but should not be attempted until the situation is under control, and the sentiments are genuine.
- Ask for help. There is support and advice from anti-bullying charities.

If you want to minimize the risks of your child becoming a bully:

- Explain how teasing and name calling can make someone feel, and point out that these are 'mild' forms of bullying which can escalate.
- Examine your own parenting style. If you use intimidation or threats to maintain discipline, you dramatically increase your son's chances of using similar techniques.
- Furnish him with the skills to resolve conflicts non-violently and to express himself well.
- Discuss what happens if you stand by while bullying goes on. Nearly three-quarters of bullying is done in groups. Discuss ways to act if he is part of a crowd in which bullying takes place. How can he resist group pressure? What can he say to a friend who is bullying? ('I like you but I don't like what you are doing' has been highly recommended.)
- Find ways to channel his energy and aggression. Sports and physically strenuous play can help him to release pent-up energy and to learn self-control. However, make sure sport is under supervision, at least at first.

- Has your son got enough to keep him challenged and occupied? Believe it or not, some kids bully because they have nothing better to do.

■ CASE STUDY – Jan and Paul's story

Bullying often starts with name calling and escalates into something far more ominous. Boys are reluctant to tell their parents and often try to handle the situation alone until the burden becomes too great, as you can see from Steven's story.

Steven was systematically bullied for three years between the ages of eleven and fourteen, and his parents, Jan and Paul McFarlane had no idea. 'It started gradually, and just escalated. Steven was always very good at pretending, covering things up. There was no reason to question him until the bullies really got to him. When we found out, we were devastated. It set off terrible flashbacks to when I was bullied at school,' says Paul.

The McFarlanes knew that Steven's school in Hartlepool had a reputation but a new anti-bullying policy and assurances that bullies would not be tolerated assuaged their fears. However, things were to get worse.

'His schoolwork was being defiled or his school clothes were ripped up and torn. He always claimed it was an accident. I used to berate him for being so careless,' says Jan.

The couple started to notice a change in Steven's behaviour. 'He was always very calm and polite, quite studious. Suddenly, he was very aggressive in his manner. He would come home, slam the door and run upstairs to his bedroom, without any conversation,' says Paul.

Yet the bullying didn't stop at name calling and soon Steven was coming home with bruising and marks. Nonetheless he still ruled out foul play. It was not until Steven received a neck injury forcing him to wear a neck brace for weeks that things took on a new and sinister turn. 'The bullies bounced him upside down on his head with his neck taking the full force. He collapsed. He could easily have been killed,' says Jan. Incredibly, the school claimed that Steven had been involved in a fight. The McFarlanes knew this was implausible, and that Steven was not a violent child. 'We immediately became suspicious and confronted him. It was a massive turning point for Steven. He could not keep it to himself any longer. He just broke down in tears and confessed to being targeted,' says Jan.

The couple began to log each and every bullying incident and informed the school, but the official line was that they were dealing with it. 'We felt extremely frustrated and guilty that we were failing Steven,' says Paul.

One day the bullies beat Steven up – the school described it as a 'fun fight'. 'It was the last straw. Steven was in a terrible state – even hospital doctors reacted in astonishment. His face was black and blue with cuts all over, his nose was broken and still pouring with blood two hours after the fight,' explained Paul.

Steven was forced to have six weeks' convalescence at home but during that time, he became increasingly aggressive and intolerant. At their wits' end, the McFarlanes sought out an educational social worker. 'She counselled Steven and liaised with the school on our behalf. We also reported the assault as GBH [grievous bodily harm] to the police,' says Jan.

Two months later Steven was awarded £100 in damages from the court and one boy was excluded from school, albeit for only three days.

'We wanted the school to act far more responsibly, so we contacted our local MP for Hartlepool, Peter Mandelson. Suddenly, the school wanted to talk to us. Steven was given a special pass to safeguard him against the bullies. Whenever he felt in danger he could leave the school or classroom. It seemed to work,' says Jan.

Virtually overnight, the bullying stopped but the McFarlanes were still worried about its after-effects on Steven and on their family. 'We had felt like the only parents to suffer, and felt desperate that other parents avoid the devastation bullying can cause to families,' says Paul.

As a result, Jan and Paul launched the support group, Families Against Bullying (FAB), and together with local theatre groups, they tackle the issue. 'It's really opened our eyes to how widespread bullying is. In school workshops we talk to kids or discuss with parents what action should be taken to stamp out bullying. The response is always overwhelming,' says Jan.

10

Encouraging positive behaviour

Sometimes, parenting can feel like a them-against-us battle. In the heat of the everyday 'Pick it up', 'Don't do that', 'I won't tell you again' versus the 'Why do I have to?', 'It's not fair', and 'You can't make me' rigmarole, it is all too easy to lose sight of the fact that family life is supposed to be fulfilling.

When you feel like you are fighting an uphill battle simply to get your son to listen to you or to lend a hand, take a step back and remind yourself that your children are not on this earth with the sole mission of making life difficult for you. Intrinsically, they want to please you and be cooperative. If you have done all the right things in his infancy, i.e. kept him clean, fed and watered, and given him love and affection, then in his later life, despite all evidence to the contrary, your son is 'attached' to you, and essentially wants to please you. Better still, with the right approach, this willing nature can be coaxed from the most unlikely contenders – so never give up hope. It seems that the key to encouraging good behaviour in your son is to build on his natural desire to please.

Nevertheless, before you start turning cartwheels of joy around the room, there is one cautionary note to be struck. However effective your encouraging positive behaviour strategies may be, no child can be expected to behave impeccably all the time. Keep your expectations realistic and these positive behaviour tactics can really work wonders, and benefit not just you but your whole family.

The fundamentals

It seems that boys like rules, leadership and structure more than girls. In the *Leading Lads* report, 71 per cent of boys with high self-esteem believed that their parents 'lay down the right rules' as compared to only 41 per cent of high self-esteem girls. As if to reinforce the theory that providing structure suits boys, only 35 per cent of boys with low self-esteem approved of their parents' rules.

Consequently, setting some sort of limits and boundaries for your son is imperative. Naturally, acceptable behaviours will vary from family to family but all children require predictability of expectation and response. Not that they know that, of course. Do not expect your son to accept your rules and boundaries with a cheery 'Thanks'. Be prepared for complaints and outrage, and remember that just as he needs limitations, he also needs to butt up against them.

> My mum and dad are pretty fair and I like that because then I know where I stand.   *Fourteen-year-old*

If you are anxious that this smacks of an outmoded authoritarian approach, think again. Enforcing consistent limits shows your son that you care enough to be firm and/or compassionate as the case dictates. You may be surprised to learn that children can prosper in the harshest of disciplinary homes, provided that the parents are predictable, simply because the children know the rules and learn how to stay out of trouble. Ironically, it is when children are given complete freedom that they really feel insecure. Young people want to know that someone cares enough to stop their excesses and that they are safe. This can be especially true for sons who tend to test boundaries more willingly than girls, and who also take greater risks.

Each family will have its own idiosyncratic rules to guide their children's behaviour, but once you have decided on what works in your home, you must stick to it.

What you can do

- *First decide what is important to you.* For example, if this is your son's safety, this becomes the guiding principle behind the rules you implement, for instance your nine-year-old is allowed to cross minor roads but not the main road.

- *Choose wisely.* Rules that are based on immediate safety must never, ever be broken without dire consequences. However, rules about folding his pyjamas, for example, do not have life-threatening consequences if broken, nor will he lead an unfulfilled life if his jim-jams remain on the floor rather than under the pillow. He will, nonetheless, be unhappy if he is allowed to believe that bullying or hurting others, for example, is acceptable behaviour. Keep things in perspective and choose the rules that you must enforce wisely.

- ***Rules have to suit your son's age and behaviour.*** Rules will have to be revisited from time to time to make sure that they are still appropriate, but the guiding principle remains the same. Continuing the personal safety theme, the eleven-year-old can now go to town with his friends, but he must call to say he has arrived safely, and must be home by a set time.

- ***Clearly explain the rules you set and the principles behind them to everyone in the household.*** If your son knows what is expected of him and why it matters, he is more likely to accept and go along with your rules. You can discuss how certain rules might work in practice, but be prepared for trick questions of the 'What if I did this?' variety. Do not fall into the trap of getting caught up in debating minutiae when simply trying to reinforce your general message.

- ***Do not expect it to sink in straight away.*** You will probably have to reiterate the rules on several occasions and, if he continually flouts them, you must establish whether this is because he does not understand, he has forgotten or he plain does not like it. Remind him if it is either of the first two, and reiterate the rule in plain and simple terms and why it is important if it is the latter. If he still disobeys, you have to look at sterner action (see When Things Go Wrong, page 226).

- ***Some families put a list of the rules in a communal room.*** For instance, on the fridge once they have been discussed and agreed, as a general reminder. Whether that works for you or not, the general rule of thumb if rules are to work, is to make sure that you show your pleasure when they are followed, and are firm when they are broken.

- **Encourage him to view rules as agreements between you.** As such, he is less likely to break them just because he thinks he can get away with it.
- **Be consistent.** That means that you consistently stand firm and do not crumble under the torrent of protests and/or nagging. It also means consistency between you and your partner. It is no good if one of you is self-disciplined and enforces the rules but the other patently thinks that it is nonsense and ignores them.
- **Apply the rules in a way that best suits each individual child.** There may well be common sibling battles over different treatment, but if the principle behind the rule is the same, the rules can vary for each child according to age and maturity. For example, older brother has a later bedtime but both children need to be in bed in time to give them sufficient sleep.
- **Exceptions to rules.** If you make an exception, make sure that you explain why so that the general rule still holds good in the normal course of events.

Your parenting style
None of us may want to admit it but, when it comes to encouraging positive behaviour, how you behave with your children has far more influence than anything you might say.

In a nutshell, what you do should reinforce your expectations, not undermine them. Here are the three most common parenting styles and you may recognise yourself in one or more of them. Yet only one of these parenting styles is proven to be effective in encouraging positive behaviour.

Authoritarian

These parents tend to dominate their children with words or actions. They are often critical and demand obedience without discussion or explanation. They often seem angry with their children, which may stem from personal unhappiness or resentment that is redirected at the kids. They have obedient children but this is based on fear. As a result, the children may rebel as they become teenagers or, perhaps worse, remain meek and easily intimidated as they become adults.

Laissez-faire

Parents who try to cajole their children into compliance often get disobedience. These parents frequently turn a blind eye to serious misbehaviour because they do not know how to handle it or do not have the stomach for confrontation. This often leads to repressed anger and resentment. Sadly, these parents are the most likely to end up injuring their children when it all gets too much for them, and they finally snap and overreact.

Assertive

Not to be confused with aggressive parenting, these parents are usually calm with good self-esteem, and are vigilant in observing their children's behaviour and responding accordingly. They tend to accord each member of the family respect, but expect compliance with house rules.

It is not hard to spot the winner, is it? Yet, in reality, very few parents fit neatly into any one of these categories. Most parents are a queasy mixture of the first two. All too often, you back off and back off repeatedly, and then blow up and have a complete and probably extreme clampdown, which is impossible to enforce for any length of time. You may swing from one extreme to the other on the strict-soft spectrum from week to week or month to month. It is exhausting and your son has no reason to take your vows and threats seriously because he knows that in a short while you will go back to ignoring his backchat, and have given up on trying to make him tidy up.

If this pendulum behaviour is all too familiar, do not blame yourself – it is incredibly common and an easy trap to fall into. The good news is that there is a solution at hand.

What you can do

For success, much depends on how you feel about yourself. If you view parenting as a life of servitude, you are coming at it from the wrong angle. A self-sacrificing whine will not get results. You have to have a positive approach to your son and his positive behaviour. Try to always think the best of him, which is not a case of looking at life through rose-tinted spectacles, but using the self-fulfilling prophecy rule to good effect. Then, if you want your son to do as you ask, combine this with the view that you are just as important as everyone else in the household. You

> You learn that parents are not the ultimate authority – the relationship changes. *Fifteen-year-old*

cannot command respect if you do not respect yourself and the role you play.

How to get better results:

- **Mean business.** Do not wheedle and do not shout, but let it be known by your tone and body language that you expect results now.
- **If you fear conflict or are half-hearted, you will sound defeated.** This is before you even start and your son will recognize this.
- **To convey your intent, stop what you are doing.** This is often the hardest bit for time-pressed parents. Go up to your son and ask him to look at you before you speak.
- **Give your instructions clearly.** And one at a time.
- **Get an acknowledgement from him.** This is to make sure that he understands you.
- **Do not get into a debate.** If he ignores you, calmly repeat it. Do not debate or feel the need to give reasons. Be firm and stay calm, and continue to signal that you mean business and are so confident of success that you will not even get upset.
- **Do not wander off.** There may be 101 things to do, but make sure he complies before moving on.
- **A simple 'Good' or 'Thanks' will suffice.** When he complies, do not crumple and thank him profusely or he will think that being obedient is something extraordinary.

The above method is time-consuming initially, and time is the one thing that most parents lack. Nevertheless, it is

Devious defiance

Although parents often associate adolescence with open defiance, most teenagers would prefer to avoid the direct disobedience approach. This does not mean that they do not intend to defy you, but they would rather be more devious about it.

If confronted with a rule that he does not like, rather than openly flout it, your teenage son is more likely to try to skirt round it with half-truths and deviousness – and his friends may be brought into the deception too.

Therefore, with this in mind, it is important to make sure that you leave no scope for misinterpretation when laying down the rules. If your instructions are not adequately clear from the outset, your son will conspire – often with the collusion of his mates – to slip off the hook with glib excuses.

Always confront your son if he disobeys you. However, if you want to maintain a degree of control over his actions, you must be clear and unambiguous in the beginning, and give him less scope for defiance.

effective in the long run and worth the effort. Once your son gets used to this no-nonsense approach, he will comply more readily and it will take less time until eventually he does as you say without question (most of the time, anyway).

Arguing and bargaining

If you are only half-hearted when you issue instructions, your son will come up with a dozen reasons to take absolutely no notice of what you have just asked him to do. This prevaricating takes place for two main reasons. At its most basic level, he uses reasoning and bargaining to buy himself some time. While quibbling over pedantics with you, he has managed to watch the next quarter of an hour of his favourite programme. Since there is only fifteen minutes left and you have let him watch the first half, you might as well give in and let him watch to the end. Sound familiar?

By his adolescent years, your son has experienced that rules can be bent, and that adults do not operate in black and white but in various shades of grey. He will try it on to see how far he can go.

A less overt cause for challenging your decisions is to see if you mean what you say. What does it take to make you change your mind? In a young person's erratic logic, if you can be easily talked out of a decision, do you really mean it when you say 'I love you' or will you change your mind about that too?

By getting drawn into an argument based on your son's inconsistent logic, you are giving the message that you are not in control, and that you accept any old argument as a basis for discussion. If you are going to argue, make sure the argument is based on adult logic at least.

Rebellion or challenging authority. It starts at your parents and then comes to the world at large.

Seventeen-year-old

Easier still, avoid all the time-wasting by using the above positive behaviour techniques (pages 217–8) combined with the useful 'Do it now and we'll discuss it later' approach. One parent recommends using the 'Three strikes and out' method. She will readily answer three 'Why?' questions before she plays her 'Because I say so' card. This allows her son to get a rational explanation but also cuts short any diversions into the realms of surrealism. It is one of the rules she always sticks to and, because he knows that, he tends to keep the procrastinating short.

Keeping it going
The hardest thing of all about encouraging positive behaviour and effective discipline is that it is relentless and you are only human. There will always be times when you give in to your son too easily because you just do not have the energy to resist. It is not great, but it happens. However, it is important that you do not get dispirited and stop trying to stand firm. If you keep these lapses to a minimum, your positive behaviour initiative will not grind to a halt. It might bump along for a while, but it will recover and it is not such a bad thing for your son to learn that you are fallible.

The problem for children who have 'perfect' parents who grant their every wish is that when these kids meet 'real life', it can be a genuine shock to them. Realizing that injustices happen and that adversity needs to be faced up to is safer learned at the hands of those who love you rather than from a cruel world. If you have the odd bad day, your son will soon learn the useful social and survival skill of knowing when to be assertive, and when to back off. Similarly, if you occasionally fly off the handle, have an irrational outburst or cannot do all

Attention Deficit Hyperactivity Disorder

Attention Deficit Hyperactivity Disorder (ADHD) is a condition where children find it very difficult to focus their attention or control their behaviour. They cannot concentrate for long and they often do or say things on impulse without thinking.

Estimates vary but about one to three in one hundred children have ADHD, and it is more common in boys than girls.

What are the signs of ADHD?

These behaviours usually start during the toddler stage and always before he reaches six or seven years old. ADHD can be present in varying degrees of severity and is sometimes found together with dyslexia. However, just because a child is naughty or defiant, it does not necessarily mean he has ADHD. Children who have ADHD are:

- Restless and cannot sit still or do one thing for very long.
- Easily distracted.
- May appear careless and slapdash because of an inability to pay attention.
- May find it hard to wait their turn or to listen when someone is talking to them.
- Disruptive in play.
- Irritating to other children and find it hard to make friends.

- Unable to concentrate on schoolwork and fall behind.

What you can do

Children with ADHD can be very challenging and hard to manage. They are exhausting for parents and siblings, and the whole family can become stressed which, in itself, leads to further problems.

- Talk to your son's teacher or school nurse.
- See your doctor who may refer you to a child and adolescent psychiatrist or a paediatrician. Medication may be prescribed.
- Make sure you eliminate all other possible explanations for the behaviour, such as upset or violence at home, learning difficulties, hearing/speech impairment, physical/sexual abuse.
- Training in behavioural therapies and strategies are helpful to the whole family. You will need strategies to help him to learn to concentrate so that he is not dependent on drugs in the long term.
- Counselling for the family or individual members may be available.

For more information, contact the YoungMinds Parents' Information Service on 0800 018 2138, which can give you details of available help and how to find it locally.

that your demanding son requires of you, so be it. He will cope and he may learn that although life may not always go as he would like, he will get by, just as you do.

It is best to accept that you will not be able to get it right all the time. You may fall off the 'positive behaviour' bandwagon from time to time, but here are a few hints to tip the odds in your favour when trying to integrate positive behaviour techniques into your parenting style.

- ***Concentrate on the positive.*** Tell your son what to do rather than what not to do. Any phrase prefaced with 'Don't you dare ...' is heading for confrontation, and may even put ideas in his head.
- ***Be precise.*** Tell him to 'Get your coat and bag, we're leaving now' rather than 'Hurry up, we're going to be late'.
- ***Allow enough time.*** Just think of morning hysteria and you know that you raise the stakes when you are rushing against the clock.
- ***Public face-saving.*** To avoid shaming or embarrassing your son in front of others, pre-warn him that you expect him to comply when you tell him 'It's time to go' or whatever set of behaviour you expect. Then, if he starts to complain you can remind him of what you agreed, and indicate that you expect compliance without any further fuss.
- ***Use humour.*** Older boys in particular respond well to humour. If you look like you are on the brink of a confrontation, see if you can find a way to drolly show him how ludicrous and futile resistance would be. Make sure he knows you are poking fun at the situation

rather than him or your jolly jape could backfire sensationally.

- **Choices.** With younger boys, you can give them two options, both of which you are happy with. For example, 'Do you want broccoli or carrots with your pasta?' gives him a choice, but no vegetables at all is not an option.

- **Consequences.** In some cases, you can pass the decision making to your son so that he learns the consequences of making choices. For instance, 'If you stay on the play-station there will be no time to play penalties before your shower. Are you staying on it or coming out?' When boys realize there are consequences to their decisions, they become more self-reliant and self-disciplined. Much better than a flat command to 'Come off that play-station now'.

Teamwork

If you are in a partnership, it is very important that you support each other in encouraging positive behaviour and in enforcing rules.

The problem for mothers with boys in particular, is that boys realize sometime around puberty that they are bigger and stronger than their mother, and that she can no longer physically make them do things. This dawning realization is usually accompanied by a son giving his mother a lot of backchat, being disrespectful, particularly in front of his friends, and generally taking little notice of what she says.

At this point, it helps if the mother's partner (or any other adult for that matter) steps in and quotes that old chestnut,

'Don't speak to your mother like that.' It is not that a mother cannot handle this on her own, she most certainly can – if nothing else, she can always resort to bargaining with the services she provides. But it is useful for your son to learn that his mother and father respect and support each other. By stressing that he must respect and be polite to his mum, your son learns how people should relate to each other in a partnership, and this can help him socially and as he forms his own early relationships.

However, if a male partner is going to step in to lend support when the mother is enforcing rules, it is imperative that his role is to calm the situation down or to tell the boy not to be rude etc., but not to take over the situation. The problem still has to be resolved between the son and his mother otherwise the male partner's well-intentioned intervention will only serve to undermine the mother's position in the house. Naturally, the same is true if the mother backs up her male partner during an altercation between him and their son.

When things go wrong

Despite your best efforts, there will be times when your son oversteps the mark and behaves badly. Using positive encouragement techniques will minimize these occasions but, like it or not, there will always be times when you need to use some form of discipline.

Understandably, the well-chosen constructive words of correction that you run through your head in quieter moments do not always come to mind first. More often than not, when things do go horribly wrong, you become so incensed by whatever he has done that your best intentions fly out of the window, and your first angry reaction is to lash out either verbally or physically. He then feels wretched or possibly defiant and confrontational, in which case the whole thing escalates still further, and you momentarily feel better and then, in an instant, you feel guilty.

It is a common and counterproductive approach to discipline that rarely achieves more than to make you feel fleetingly good, and then bad for quite some time.

The best kind of discipline involves, in a measured and fair way, giving your son the information that he needs to put things right and to model his behaviour in future. Does this sound impossibly smug and unreal? Perhaps, but read on. If you give some thought to the following strategies and pitfalls, then the next time he sends you up the wall, try implementing the ones that feel right for you, your son and the particular situation you find yourselves in, and see if you get better results.

Challenging unacceptable behaviour

To do this successfully, you need to get into the habit of describing what you see and how it makes you feel without name calling or labelling. Point out the effect his action has on you/the family, for instance it creates extra work for you, and ask him to find another way of dealing with the problem. This approach makes your son face up to the consequences of his actions and gives him an opportunity to do things differently without losing face. And if you can manage to do this in a firm but calm way he is far less likely to react in the normal defensive, knee-jerk reaction that you get from a confrontational, all-shouting and thumping approach.

Yellow card

Sometimes, you will feel that his misdemeanour requires some sort of action on your part. If you decide to impose a punishment, it is important to give your son due warning rather than to impose retribution out of the blue.

By using a yellow card system or some variant thereof, your son has tangible evidence of your intention to act if he does not start behaving. Whereas, if you do not give any prior warning, he has no chance to behave better.

That does not mean that you should go down the route of saying, 'If you do that one more time, I'll ...' ad infinitum, where both you and he know that you will never carry it out. You both need to know that the yellow card is a last warning and you will act swiftly if he does not conform.

The benefit of the yellow card system is that once its significance is understood, it avoids you having to go into details about what will happen next if he does not comply. He will know very clearly what the repercussions are and in this way he will feel that he is taking responsibility for his actions and decisions.

Sanctions

Although most parents dislike the idea of having to use sanctions, realistically they are effective and, as a result, they are used in the majority of households.

Nevertheless, you should only threaten a sanction or punishment if you mean it because, to have any credibility at all, you must carry it out once the threat is made. Which leads neatly on to say that your threat must be practical. Do not say, 'If you carry on arguing, we're going to turn around and go straight home' when you have just crossed the English Channel and are on your way to the south of France because it is patently a threat that is not going to be implemented.

In addition, try to remember that a sanction imposed on your son is not supposed to punish you too. If you are going to ban him from the play-station for a week, make sure that it is not at a time when you need peace and quiet in order to work, because you will hear plenty of grumbling for the next few days.

Make the punishment fit the crime
Sanctions are not supposed to be pleasant, but they should never be harmful or overly severe. The closer the link between the action and the sanction, the easier it is for your son to understand. Thus, 'If you hit your brother with that drumstick, I'll take it away and you can't play your drums today' makes more sense than 'If you hit your brother with that drumstick, you won't go to Mark's house on Saturday'.

Since sanctions do not always make it clear why the problem behaviour has to stop, it can be useful to discuss the incident with your son once the situation has calmed down, and to see how such a confrontation could be avoided next time. Some of the most common sanctions parents report using include:

- Sending to bed early (sounds absurdly old-fashioned but it apparently works).
- Uninviting friends who are booked to come and play – not a good idea if it is an unfamiliar guest but okay if he's always at your house or is part of the problem.

- Deprivation of privileges – particularly effective for older siblings.
- Banning a favourite TV programme – hard to enforce if he has a television in his room.

Show your feelings

If your son has done something that makes you extremely angry, you should tell him so in no uncertain terms. You need to show him your feelings and let him see that you are not some kind of robot. If you must shout, and most of us do when we are angry or about to lose our grip on sanity, then try to return to a quieter voice as soon as possible.

Older children and adolescents have a very strong sense of hypocrisy and they will know if you are pretending that everything is fine and dandy when under the surface you are quietly seething. Better to get your feelings out in the open, in as controlled a fashion as possible, and this should help you to deal honestly with problems together in the future.

Know when to stop

Once you have made your point and got your message across, the grown-up thing to do is to let it go and move on. Unfortunately, the grown-up thing to do is often the hardest and more often you may find yourself entering the realms of the 'And another thing …' kingdom. At this point, it is almost guaranteed that your son will stop listening to you.

The trick is to recognize the point at which you begin to overstate your case and to stop.

Bribery

There are few parents who have not resorted to bribery out of desperation at one time or another. However, you have to be aware that this is a high risk option because, if overused, your son will soon learn to raise the stakes. The quick learner may also turn it against you and start saying that he will only do what you ask if you do something for him or reward him in some way. The biter bit, as they say.

Time out

This is a good solution when you need to create space between warring factions in the house, and when you need a little time to gather your thoughts and decide what to do next. It is also a valuable safety measure if you feel that you are about to lose control.

Once each child is in a separate room you can speak to them individually and each child has an opportunity to think about what has happened, what he might have done wrong, and how he might put this right.

Many parents send a badly behaved boy to his bedroom until he is ready to cooperate and apologize, others choose a more quiet and boring place for the miscreant to ponder his misdemeanours. Either way, it is a good method to build some space between your son and a very heated situation.

The danger that some parents report with time out is that once in his bedroom, if a boy is still very angry or feels his banishment is a miscarriage of justice, he may become disruptive and wreck the room or start peeling off the wallpaper, for example. This understandably makes the parents even angrier and escalates the situation somewhat.

Smacking

The stark reality is that the vast majority of parents profess a dislike of smacking and yet 91 per cent of parents smack their children. It is a conundrum. Either someone is telling fibs or we smack our children in spite of our best intentions.

Put bluntly, all the evidence shows that smacking is ineffectual. Children who are hit learn to hit others, tend to be more aggressive, may be more prone to depression, and it is even suggested that physical punishment can reduce intelligence.

In 2002, Elizabeth Thompson Gershoff of Columbia University reviewed eighty-eight studies on smacking, involving 36,000 children, and data covering sixty-two years. She found that children aged ten to twelve were harmed the most by smacking. This may be because naughtiness at this age angers parents more than that of younger children, for whom parents have lower expectations. Or it may be because children of this age are rarely hit, and so react more strongly when it happens.

Other findings include:

- Most smacking occurs between 5 p.m. and bedtime.
- Boys are smacked more than girls.
- Children aged five to eight are smacked the hardest.
- Parents who get on badly with each other are more likely to smack.
- Parents with big families are more likely to smack.

Thompson Gershoff also analysed the link between smacking, child behaviour, and antisocial adults. Smacking was associated with only one desirable form of behaviour – increased immediate compliance.

This analysis of the research on smacking supports what most parents in their heart of hearts already know – your son is more likely to get a smack because you're feeling tired, angry or stressed, rather than because he is behaving particularly badly. Lashing out is more often a response to your state of mind and stress levels, and not a response to what your son has done wrong. Perhaps this is why parents so often feel guilty after smacking a child – subconsciously they realize that they did not smack because they considered it the right thing to do, but because they were feeling wretched.

Once you can admit this to yourself, it is much easier to curb the impulse to lash out, and to find a less excessive way to curtail your child's bad behaviour. It is worth remembering that even if you have never raised your hand to your son, you can still do damage. If you self-righteously congratulate yourself on never smacking your son, but systematically and cruelly tear him apart with a good tongue lashing, do not forget that this can be just as terrorizing and humiliating in its way.

■ **PROBLEM SOLVING**
There are times when I want to hurt my child
You should stop smacking your son immediately if at any time:

- It becomes your first choice of punishment rather than a last resort.
- It makes you feel good.
- It happens frequently or more often than you would like.

- You feel he deserves it because you were smacked as a child.
- You ever hit him so hard that you leave a mark or a bruise.

If any of the above apply to you, you need to reconsider your actions, pull yourself up short and stop smacking now.

If you think you have a more serious problem and you may actually be beating your child and not just smacking, you must stop the hitting immediately. This is tantamount to physical abuse and could be considered a criminal act. Talk to your doctor or phone a helpline such as the NSPCC or ChildLine. You need some help and, most importantly, so does your child.

■ PROBLEM SOLVING

My son winds me up all the time

Some parents believe that they have a troublesome son who goes out of his way to be difficult, and to wind them up. They describe how there is always an atmosphere of conflict in the family and that they have got to the stage where they do not even like him any more. The whole family is living under the oppressive cloud of a destructive parent-son relationship.

Although this sounds extreme, it is not so far from the truth for many families. Dr Dinah Jayson, a child and adolescent consultant psychiatrist at the Trafford Trust, explains:

Children are very sensitive to their parents' moods, often responding with behavioural problems which make the situation worse. The relationship between you and your child becomes strained, and before you know it, everyone is caught up in a vicious circle of unhappiness, with you and your child growing further and further apart. This unhelpful pattern causes further stress in itself, so it can persist even when the original source of stress has gone away. If you don't realise that this is happening, it is easy to get into the habit of criticism and blame, and this in itself can become a problem for the whole family.

The root of the problem is that all children need your undivided attention on a regular basis and, if it is not given proactively by you, then they seek it in other ways. Therefore, if you are busy and time is at a premium, your son may only get your attention when he misbehaves. Before you protest, let's be honest here, how often do you reward your son when he is quietly absorbed in some activity? Indeed you may not even notice and so the 'difficult' son becomes troublesome in order to get your attention because even negative attention is better than being ignored. Not only that, but negative attention is usually immediate and undivided – two of the most highly desirable qualities for all children. And the net result? You end up believing that you are a lousy parent and that you have got a bad child who is out to get you.

At this point you have to take a step back and separate the person from the problem. With the minimum of effort, you can probably predict when your son is most likely to be difficult and to make your life hell and, naturally, it is at pressurized times. Perhaps it is getting ready for school in the morning when you are all in a rush, maybe it is on a rainy day when you are all stuck indoors. Could it be when your son is playing with other rowdy boys without enough adult supervision?

You have now identified when trouble is most likely to happen. Next, take a look at the exceptions – remind yourself of times when your son has behaved well. Not so easy perhaps, but persevere because even the worst child has moments when he is good although you may not normally notice because you are expecting the worst. Ask yourself what was happening then? What was the difference?

Slowly you can build up a picture of when trouble occurs and when it is held at bay and why, and you slowly realize that you can influence whether or not you allow trouble to shape your lives or not.

Establish the 'trouble black spots' – maybe it is when he is tired after school and his aggravating big sister is on his case while you are in the kitchen, or is he at his worst when his free time is unstructured? Now you can start to eliminate those occasions or at least acknowledge these problem times with him, and give him some assurance that he is going to get some protected special time with you. You can also start praising or treating good behaviour and even request particular behaviour in return for extra rewards, for instance putting his school bag on the hook (make it something precise and tangible – tidying his room is too vague).

When he has less cause to act up to get your attention, you can start to see him in a more positive light once again. He really is a nice boy who is trying hard. He, in turn, can see himself as a warrior fighting trouble (see page 136). Consequently, rather than he and you 'fighting', you can join forces, ganging up together and fighting against trouble. This will build the positive relationship that you both want.

Armed with this mental (or written) diary of occasions when trouble occurs and when peace reigns, it is easy to see that your son has not been winding you up deliberately. Rather, you are all victims of a vicious circle of circumstances that reinforce bad behaviour. Once identified for what it is, you will feel empowered to know that you and your son are in the driving seat, and that it is up to you whether you allow circumstances to control your relationship or whether you take control.

Whatever actions you take, one thing is certain. Your son is not 'out to get you'. He may even think that you are 'out to get him' because no matter how hard he tries, you only notice the bad behaviour, and he might as well not bother. It does not have to be like this. He needs to know that you do notice the good and that you care. After a while, you will see a positive difference.

Once you know why a child misbehaves, you should understand that it is not a personal vendetta against you. Try to think the best of him and give him a chance to shine.

■ CASE STUDY – Charlie's story

Dr Dinah Jayson has drawn on her experience as a child and adolescent psychiatrist to pull together a case study that is an amalgam of the many families that she sees:

Charlie is in trouble at school and at home. His parents are at the end of their tether and don't know what to do. The school is threatening to exclude Charlie because he has been hitting other children.

'The typical thing to look at is what led up to his behaviour. Has he always been like this or is it a recent thing?'

The family

Charlie is eleven. He has a younger sister of nine who is as good as gold. He has loving parents. There is an uncle who has had alcohol problems and another uncle with specific learning difficulties and a cousin who has similar behaviour problems to himself.

The background

Charlie has always been on the go since he could walk. He is into everything and never sits still – a real live wire. He is full of beans and really quick to respond, a fun kid to be around but very wearing for his parents. He has never been able to play quietly and has trouble concentrating on one activity.

The family tried a behavioural group for parents of kids with behaviour problems when Charlie was younger. This helped a little, but although Jane, the mother, still tries to use these skills, she is so worn down by it all that she has largely given up trying.

At school, Charlie blurts out the answers before his class-mates and is always getting into trouble because he cannot sit still and is easily distracted. At home, he is accident prone and clumsy. He tries hard, but mess and trouble always seem to surround him, and he does not really understand why.

Charlie's troubles are mounting. People are not inviting him to parties because parents find him too hard to handle, and do not want him around. His work at school is slapdash, disorganized and unfinished. He is not unpopular because his antics amuse the other kids, but he has no close friends. His family does not take him on outings any more because he is hard work. In addition, his grandma allows his sister to come and stay but not Charlie because she cannot cope with his boisterous behaviour.

The crisis

Until now, Charlie has had an experienced teacher who could just about handle him. The school has used incentive schemes to good effect, but he now has a young and inexperienced teacher, and she is finding it very difficult to cope with a class of thirty-two and Charlie.

As Charlie gets older and more and more excluded from things, he becomes more miserable and attracts more trouble. This is adversely affecting his relationship with his parents and his peers at school. He starts lashing out. He is now on a warning for his behaviour.

The school thinks that the parents are not doing enough and the parents blame the school. Meanwhile, the grandparents think that Charlie's parents are too lax and this has caused a family rift, which puts additional pressure on Jane who is getting a little depressed. She thinks that it is all her fault and that she is doing something wrong. She feels like she has tried everything and it has not worked.

The school nurse finds nothing wrong with Charlie and the special needs coordinator thinks the family is at fault.

Jane meets up with a friend who she has not seen for a long time. They talk and the friend explains that her son has Attention Deficit Hyperactivity Disorder (ADHD), and recommends that Jane gets Charlie assessed.

The treatment
Charlie goes to the child psychiatrist. The school and family fill in a series of questionnaires. These show that throughout Charlie's life there has been a record of overactivity, inattention, and impulsivity. This is handicapping because it is leading to social exclusion for him, and for his family as well.

The child psychiatrist diagnoses ADHD, having excluded learning difficulties and various other physical causes. There have been no deaths or negative life events that can account for the escalating seriousness of the situation.

Charlie's behaviour has been getting steadily worse and it came to a head because of the inexperienced teacher, and because Charlie's parents are concerned about how he will cope in secondary school.

Thus, having excluded any other causes and established that Charlie has a caring family, the child psychiatrist concludes that he has ADHD, and decides to put him on a trial course of Ritalin. This is a stimulant medication that aims, figuratively speaking, to put a thought bubble in his head so that he stops and thinks before he acts.

Charlie has a trial at a low dose for a week, then at a higher dose for a second week, and an even higher dose for a third week. This is done in conjunction with the school and parents, who monitor his behaviour to see whether it makes a difference. The observations are:

- First week – cannot tell, not very clear.
- Second week – fair improvement, but not sure because of Grandma's visit whether medication was the cause.
- Third week – the improvement is sustained.

The effects
The school is amazed at the results. Charlie is like a different child. Before, he was automatically blamed because he was so often in trouble. The culture of blame is removed and Charlie responds well.

Charlie's mum is less depressed as she sees his improvement. She starts feeling better about herself and her ability to deal with her son. She starts implementing the behavioural techniques that she learned years before and that also has a positive effect.

The child psychologist stresses the importance of using positive rewards for good behaviours, and that the medication in itself is not the answer.

Charlie wants to know why he is different from the other kids. The child psychiatrist explains that he has got ADHD – that he is affected by trouble, which is almost like an outside entity that creeps up on him when there is a lot of distraction, outside noise or if he does not want to do something. This troublesome character makes him do things that seem fun at the time, but that he has not thought through, and these actions get him into trouble.

The child psychiatrist says ADHD is a little like having a lazy police officer in your brain. Normally, a police officer regulates the traffic in your brain, but if she is not doing her job properly, then any distractions that come along take the attention of the ADHD person so that they cannot control their concentration.

One way of helping the police officer to do her job properly is to give medication to wake the police officer up. In addition, Charlie can fight this trouble that keeps visiting him because Charlie does not enjoy trouble. He is fed up with being yelled at by his parents for being naughty when he does not really understand what he has done wrong. As a result, child and family decide to set up a system where they all gang up on trouble together. It is too big for Charlie to fight on his own.

Charlie and his parents notice that he gets into more trouble if he is upset or if he has been told off because he thinks, 'Well, why bother, everyone is yelling at me anyway.' He notices that he is much better at keeping trouble at bay when he has more attention, and more direction to his activities – when he is not left to his own devices.

His parents decide to gang up on trouble by structuring his day more clearly and by being very clear on what the house rules are, and setting up a reward system for particular behaviours.

By the same token, his parents are aware that when they shout at him, Charlie is worse. They agree that they too will leave trouble outside. The next time Charlie is troublesome, they do not send him to his room and call him a naughty boy. They say to Charlie, 'Go outside the room and leave trouble outside, and then come back in again.' Similarly, Jane now feels able to say to Charlie, 'I'm in the grip of trouble and I'm going to go out of the room and leave trouble behind, and come back into the room and talk to you when I can do that without getting cross.'

The outcome

There is then a meeting between the school, the child psychiatrist, the parents, and Charlie to try to catch the times when trouble sneaks in the most in this environment. They notice that it usually happens during his unstructured time, play times mainly. They also notice that he is particularly hyperactive during school celebrations when plenty of sweets and fizzy drinks are around.

They decide between them that during play time and lunchtime, Charlie is going to join school clubs. He is on a monitoring system where he gets immediate rewards for good behaviour. Fizzy drinks and snack foods are banned. In particular, his young teacher is given advice on how to keep him focused on the task in hand. An emphasis is placed on giving positive attention and rewards for appropriate behaviours.

Effectively, Charlie gets quite excited about this because he wants to beat the trouble, and he is pleased that people are on his side to beat this together. His grandma is also involved because she takes him on special outings in return for a certain number of smiley stickers on his reward chart.

The medication he is on now has had an effect, but the whole change in perception of Charlie by the school and his parents, together with decreased blame and Jane feeling better, all contribute.

Charlie is no longer someone that people want to exclude. He starts making more friends. He used to think that he was really stupid because he never finished any tasks, but his work has improved as well. As a consequence, he is a much happier boy. His behaviour improves so much that he is no longer under threat of suspension.

The future

Charlie stays on Ritalin for the next few years. He has to have his height and weight monitored regularly to check that the dosage is correct. He is reviewed regularly every month, but once settled this becomes every six months.

There is every chance that Charlie will come off the medication in adolescence. While on medication, he learns how to make friends and carry out other appropriate social interactions. Before, he could not concentrate long enough to learn these skills. Even if Charlie is still a bit capricious when he comes off medication, at least now he has the skills to cope socially.

It turns out that Charlie's cousin also has ADHD and he too benefits from treatment.

11

Encouraging self-reliance and responsibility

As a parent, your ultimate goal is to turn out a responsible, self-confident and self-reliant offspring who goes bravely and optimistically into the wider world as an independent young adult, while still maintaining a loving and close relationship with you and the family. A good result, if you can get it.

The biggest stumbling block to achieving such an ambition is not your gauche, self-conscious son but you, in the shape of your natural desire to protect him. If you refuse to let him make his way in the big wide world on his own two feet, then he does not stand much chance of becoming an independent adult. And, when the chips are down, you have had so much practice at the protection game, that it is hard to back off and let your teenage son make his own decisions, and to follow his own path. In fact, how much freedom you give your teenager is one of the biggest causes of friction between parents and their adolescent kids.

Although it is easy, if somewhat trite, to say that the answer is to encourage self-reliance from a young age, there is more than a modicum of truth in this statement. If you have engendered a degree of self-reliance in your son from about the age of eight, you are far better placed to judge what he is capable of as an adolescent. This can help you to strike a balance between granting him more liberty to experience life outside the family, and stepping in to prevent him from coming to harm. However, most parents find it very hard to let go of the reins or to judge when children are capable of doing certain tasks for themselves.

Developing self-reliance

Families seem to vary considerably in the levels of self-reliance that they expect or encourage in their children. You may approach the topic with the attitude that your nine-year-old son is now old enough to do something for himself, so let him get on with it. Meanwhile, others may grumble a great deal about how little their son does to help out but, in reality, do very little to actively change the situation. After all, although you would like him to do things for himself, it is hard to be patient while he learns the necessary skills and, actually, it is quicker and easier to do the job yourself.

Nonetheless, giving your son some responsibility as well as more freedom is an important part of growing up. It stands him in good stead for when he wants greater independence. Your son's attitude to increased self-reliance will vary depending on his temperament but, as a general rule of thumb, provided that you introduce responsibility for a task as a mark of his increased maturity rather than as a chore, he will be keen to try new duties. In addition, being trusted by you will be seen in general terms as a welcome development.

It's a real pain when you say, 'Can I go to the cinema with my mates?' and your parents say, 'If you're grown up enough to do that, then you're old enough to help with the washing-up and cleaning.'

Fourteen-year-old

However, a note of realism should be sounded at this point. Although kids want more independence, being responsible for domestic tasks is not as appealing as being allowed to go into town with your mates, for example. Therefore, you should definitely try to give a good mix of new responsibilities and freedoms. For instance, if you now allow your son to choose his own clothes or even to buy what he likes with his clothing allowance, the trade off is that he puts his dirty laundry in the basket rather than dumping it on the floor or that he irons his own clothes.

Taking a positive approach

Your son is far more likely to move towards growing self-reliance if his efforts are met with your appreciation, and your clear pleasure in his ability to be trusted. Even domestic chores become less onerous if you present them in a positive light. Few, if any, youngsters respond well to the 'At your age, I was doing this, that and the other for my parents' approach, which paints a picture of growing maturity as a rather dismal affair. Instead, if you encourage him to view being more capable in his everyday life as a privilege, he is more likely to adopt increasing responsibility with enthusiasm.

What you can do
The key points in a positive approach to encourage self-reliance are:

- **Be patient.** You have to go more slowly with everyday tasks and to explain carefully what may seem obvious to you. Expect initial mistakes and confusion with early skills such as cooking.
- **Give warm encouragement.** Your son is more likely to accept domestic responsibility with good grace if you are encouraging rather than critical – steer away from comments like 'You shouldn't be doing it like that'.
- **Steadily share responsibilities.** You can deliberately move away from taking absolute responsibility for all of your son's needs, and start to hand over bit by bit.
- **Give him plenty of practice.** He cannot be competent at a skill without practice – try to build in time for him to improve his skills.
- **Help him to deal with the consequences of his actions.** Part of handing over responsibility is that he will have to deal with the consequences of his actions. So, if he becomes responsible for packing his own school bag and he forgets the necessary books for school that day, he will have to face the consequences. You can support and sympathize and offer practical advice, but avoid taking a patronizing 'I told you so' approach to mishaps.

When is the right time?
Deciding when your son is ready to take on additional responsibilities and freedoms is never easy. Indeed, if you ask a

handful of parents at what age children should be allowed to do certain things, such as go shopping alone or choose their own clothes or hairstyle, you will get a wide spectrum of answers. However, parents do generally agree that maturity matters more than age.

One mother of three boys that we interviewed delegates the ironing to her sons. When the oldest boy was about eight, she introduced the concept. She would finish a huge pile of ironing and then put the iron on a cool setting. Max was then invited to iron a few T-shirts and tea towels. Once he had mastered the technique, the heat setting went up, and by eleven, he was responsible for ironing all his own clothes. And then she repeated the experience with the other sons.

On asking around, most parents seem to think that they would allow an eleven-year-old to use public transport during daylight hours, and to go to the cinema alone with friends from about the age of twelve. They reported that their sons were allowed to go out in the evening with a friend from about the age of fifteen or sixteen, if they were home by 11 p.m. Mind you, across the board, it was agreed that no matter what his age, you will not get a wink of sleep until you know that your son is back home and safely tucked up in bed.

What you can do
Here are some ideas for increased self-reliance for nine- to fourteen-year-olds to cut their teeth on, as suggested by experienced parents:

- Getting their own breakfast and tea.
- Organizing their own personal hygiene.

- Helping out with domestic tasks, such as cooking, vacuuming, stacking, emptying the dishwasher, etc.
- Going to the dentist without you.
- Choosing their own clothes or hairstyle.
- Having an allowance and handling money.
- Going on public transport.
- Helping out with younger siblings.
- Going on school trips and exchange visits.
- Organizing their own study, homework, exam revision, etc.
- Dealing with small problems, such as returning a faulty purchase or correcting a wrong food order.

■ PROBLEM SOLVING

It's always somebody else's fault

Does your son automatically blame somebody else, usually you, if he cannot find something in his room? Does he always expect somebody else to get things for him, even if he is closer? If he damages something, is his immediate response, 'It wasn't my fault'? If so, your son is suffering from the common failing, especially among boys, of avoiding responsibility.

For whatever reason, generally girls seem to be more willing to take responsibility for their belongings, and for their actions. Most boys, on the other hand, seem to have a lower sense of responsibility. To add insult to injury, they do not realize that they have upset you by expecting you to take the rap for them or to do their bidding.

How can you get your son to take more responsibility? The first step is to decide whose problem it is. If the only person who will suffer from your son's inability to take responsibility is himself, then the decision is pretty clear-cut. Let him get on with it. Nonetheless, life is never that simple. If you have a dilemma, ask yourself if you can live with the consequences of allowing your son to learn from his actions.

Once you have decided on this course, it would be mean to throw him in at the deep end. Give him a helping hand by resisting the temptation to argue and label him irresponsible, instead offer constructive support and advice. If he is taking responsibility for packing school bags and sports kit, ask him each morning, 'What do you need to take with you today?' to jog his memory, until it becomes second nature. If he has lost something, resist the temptation to turn his room upside down looking for it, but make useful suggestions about where he might look himself.

You will not see a transformation overnight but, if you persevere in letting him do things for himself, and practise acting responsibly, he will soon catch on. Of course, it may all go awry in his mid-teens when he would rather take the rap than take responsibility for anything, but at least you have sown the seeds and, with any luck, this ability to be self-reliant will resurface after the mid-teen contrary years have passed.

Home alone
One way to introduce a taste of self-reliance into your son's life is, after due consideration, to allow him to stay home alone while you pop out briefly. The general consensus from interviewed parents was that eight years old was the earliest age to introduce such measures and, even then, it depends on the individual boy's maturity. However, rather than focusing on an age at which to leave him alone, it is more important to consider, 'What does he need to know?' and 'What does he need to be able to manage?' before you leave him at all.

Since parents are increasingly reluctant to let their children out on their own, being left at home alone is one of the few remaining ways for a boy to get his first taste of self-reliance and responsibility.

Obviously, at first, it should only be for the briefest of periods, and only once specific ground rules have been firmly established. One mother described how she had set the rules on no kettles, no cooking, and no climbing, and was horrified when she came home to find all her scented candles blazing away in the grate. She immediately added no matches to the list.

The most imperative rule is that your son must not open the door to anyone, and many parents include friends in this ban, but naturally he must be able to get out in a fire (and have an alternative route in mind). If you can, put the answerphone on and tell him to pick up only if he hears your voice directing him to do so. If this option is not available to you, ask him to answer the phone and to tell the caller that you are in the bath or some other fabrication that implies you are in the house. Leave him telephone numbers to call in an emergency, even if you are only going for a brief period – it is reassuring. Your son will love the fact that you trust him in the house on his own, and will revel in his new responsibility.

Quest for freedom
You know that your adolescent son is going to demand more and more freedom as he passes through his teenage years, but it is part of the nature of all adolescents that he will on occasions demand more than he expects to get – or even necessarily wants. Do not be afraid to say an unequivocal 'No' sometimes. He will naturally protest but some requests are so patently ludicrous that there really is little point in even

The cotton wool generation

It is far from easy for parents to assess the level of danger facing their children, but the two overwhelming causes of concern seem to be the risk from road traffic, and violence from strangers. In fact, since the early 1970s, although the weight of road traffic has increased considerably, the number of fatalities up to the fifteen years' age range from traffic accidents fell by over 50 per cent. Moreover, there was no increase in the extremely low number of children who were killed by strangers.

Nonetheless, the intensive media coverage of the few tragic incidents of abduction has inflamed our collective national belief that there is an increased risk to our children from 'stranger danger'. Sadly, children are statistically more at risk of injury or death from people they know, including their family.

Although parents reluctantly admit that their concerns are out of all proportion with the laws of statistical probability, an understandable if irrational fear of abduction, molestation, and danger from traffic

entering into a discussion. A flat refusal will suffice and do not even pretend that there is any room for argument. He is probably only testing you anyway and knows he does not stand a cat in hell's chance of being taken seriously.

Nonetheless, over-restrictive, and over-protective parents are a serious cause for complaint in early and mid-adolescence. Interestingly, it was the boys with low self-esteem in accidents means that none of us are prepared to take a risk with our own children.

Unfortunately, there are unwished for consequences from these protective overreactions:

- Boys are no longer allowed to walk or cycle to school and are dependent on parents to ferry them about in the car, thus denying them the opportunity for physical exercise and to learn skills of self-reliance.
- Boys no longer play outside and so they miss out on the opportunity to mix with other kids of all ages without the influence of some adult presence.
- Boys tend to play with small groups of parentally approved, same age friends, without the benefits of learning the social skills required to play with older and younger kids from different backgrounds or to settle disputes and relationships on their own.
- Boys lack the ability to travel independently and are less 'street-wise'.

the *Leading Lads* survey who complained most strongly that 'my parents treat me like a baby', whereas 70 per cent of Can-do Boys reported that 'my parents like me to make my own decisions'.

The typical head-on collisions between parents and teenagers, as depicted in numerous television sit-coms, are born of the time-honoured battle between teenagers trying to get more self-determination, and parents struggling to stay in control. Unfortunately, many families get off on the wrong foot because each holds a different interpretation of what it means to become an adult. For parents, growing up equates to taking more responsibility and living up to certain standards. For teenagers, it means being independent, making your own decisions, and running your own life. Disagreements are bound to arise as your son sees you as the enemy who is determined to thwart his quest for greater freedom, and you see him as a lazy good-for-nothing who is lounging around in your house, eating your food, and doing nothing in return. With the stage set, you come out of your corners fighting.

So, there you have it. Parents and adolescents irredeemably set at loggerheads. Well, yes and no. If you are going to get the balance right between encouraging self-sufficiency, granting greater liberty, and keeping your adolescent son safe, then you have to expect a bit of friction or even conflict along the way. Yet it does not have to dominate all of your lives. A degree of conflict is completely normal during these years. In fact, it would be odd if your teenage son did not test you to the limits on occasion. However, if you can be relatively satisfied in your own mind about what is worth fighting over and what you should let go, you will all have a much better time of it. Rules that govern personal safety must always be enforced, but it is up to you whether or not you think it is worth battling over personal choices, such as hair length and colour.

What you can do
To make sure that you keep the inevitable battles over increased self-reliance to a minimum, sort the ground rules out from the start:

- **Make it clear in which areas you intend to 'interfere'.** And which areas you will leave up to him. For example, schoolwork and his whereabouts are still your concern, but he can take charge of what he spends his pocket money on or what clothes he wears etc.
- **Accept your son for who he is.** Your son is beginning to resemble the adult he will become. It is at this time that you may start to realize that your son may not live up to your hopes or his potential, and a tinge of disappointment is the sad result. Admit this to yourself and it will help – take it out on your son, and it will not.
- **Let him make his own decisions and take the consequences.** It is hard to let your child fail, particularly if it is over something that could affect his future. Paradoxically, you have to allow your son to make mistakes just at the time when the stakes go up. If he is going to get detention for forgetting homework again, do not backtrack and help him out. However, if he is going to go to a party hosted by an unknown boy in a rough neighbourhood returning alone late at night, you might take a different view.
- **Accept your limitations.** You cannot force your towering teenager to buckle down to work, to take more responsibility or to adhere to the rules. Naturally, you can show your displeasure and impose sanctions or rewards but this may not be enough. All you can really do to get him to conform to your rules is to keep setting the boundaries, giving encouragement, and making the decisions that you think are right at the time for

the right reasons (not that you will always know what is best). And then give yourself a break – you have done your best.

- **Make yourself available.** It may be rare, but your son might occasionally ask for your advice (which he may later claim as his own good idea). You are not allowed

Parents who cannot let go

As your son approaches full independence, you begin to realize that your role as an active parent, which you have lovingly fulfilled for the past eighteen years or so, is about to disappear. Although your son still needs you, you are no longer required to give the constant care you have in the past or even to be a continuous presence. Many parents are saddened by this fact and most admit they find it hard to let go. However, a few parents find it particularly difficult, if not impossible. This is usually because of some need within yourself – maybe you are in an unhappy marriage or you have invested the entire focus of your existence in your child, or possibly your son is the only person who makes you feel emotionally fulfilled. In these circumstances, it is likely that you will still want to come first in your son's life even after he has left home.

That, of course, is an unrealistic and unfair expectation. Even teenage sons want to please their parents and you must recognize that pressure from you to stay in the nest is putting an unnecessary burden on him.

to interfere but you are expected to always be there to give support, both practical and emotional, and to get him out of sticky situations. Teenagers lack perspective and your role is to keep reinforcing the reality in a gentle and loving way.

What you can do
If you are struggling with loosening the reins, try to remember the following points:

- *Do not use emotional blackmail.* If you burden him with the feeling that he is everything to you, especially if he is an only child, you are being unfair.
- *Do not limit contacts with friends and outside activities.* Friends can never replace you but they will fulfil an important role in your son's life, and he will turn to them as confidants. If you cling on too hard, you could damage your future relationship with your son, and impair his chances of forming good friendships and meaningful relationships.
- *Get your own life.* If you have outside interests, then your son's life and his achievements will not be your sole source of satisfaction, and it also takes the pressure off him a little.
- *Do not feel sorry for yourself.* Telling him that you never see him any more in a self-pitying voice is taking advantage of his better nature. Although it may work for a while, be warned that this 'hurt' approach can lead to resentment.

- **_Try not to interfere._** It is certainly not easy to keep your nose out of his affairs, but try your best. Moreover, try even harder not to react when he accuses you of interference anyway, despite your gargantuan efforts to stay out of it. Life with a teenager is far from fair!

Curfews

Probably the biggest cause of disagreements between parents and teenage boys is the thorny issue of when he should be home. Whatever time you set, your son will resent the fact that you want to impose a curfew at all, and to him, staying out late (or, more to the point, later than you would like) is all part and parcel of being independent. Undoubtedly, you quite reasonably think that agreeing a clear-cut time by which he must be home is not only sensible but it is part of your parental duty to look out for his safety.

In fact, there is no magical hour by which you can assuredly say your sixteen-year-old 'ought' to be home. Trying to adhere rigidly to one particular time is a recipe for disaster and an open invitation to battle. Naturally during the week, you might want to be stricter about setting limits, but on weekends and during the holidays, his curfew should be something of a movable feast, dictated by circumstances and events. There may be times when, for whatever reason, you do not feel like turning out in the wee small hours, and this is just as valid as him not wanting to miss the end of a gig, for example. In reality, it is more important that you know your son's whereabouts and how he intends to get home, rather than trying to enforce an inflexible deadline. You are both better served by putting the emphasis on him being responsible enough to let you know if there is any change to plans or any problems, instead of flexing your muscles and laying down the law. That is not to say that you should not bother imposing a curfew at all – of course you should. Nevertheless, it is more important that he honours the spirit of the law and comes home sometime close to the appointed hour, rather than being in on the dot of eleven, as prescribed, and that he exercises some common sense about decisions he might have to make on the spot. For example, he may move on if he senses trouble brewing in a particular bar or get a taxi with some mates rather than wait with a gang of drunken football fans for the last bus – all prudent decisions, but they could scupper his good intention of being home on time.

What you can do

- ***Do not set curfew times in stone.*** Avoid rigidly saying that he must be home by midnight without exception. There should always be room for negotiation for special events and this helps your son to learn to discipline himself too.
- ***Reiterate that the curfew law is set.*** He may flout the law and keep coming home half an hour late, in which case you may decide to resort to threats and groundings. However, in the long run, the most effective control on your teenager is your firm insistence that the curfew stays – because this thought is constantly in his head. He may choose to ignore it but he has

> Parents should trust us: we're not stupid.
>
> *Fifteen-year-old*

to actively do so, which takes a decision on his part. Your words echoing in his head are like a little voice of conscience for your son and, despite your scepticism, it does have an effect.

- ***Do not be swayed by tantrums or bullying.*** Once you have agreed a curfew time, apart from taking certain exceptional circumstances into consideration, do not waver. He may rail at you that you are the worst parent in the world and that life is not fair, but stick to your guns and withdraw. If you believe the rule to be fair, stick to it regardless of the reaction.

- ***Lighten up.*** If the curfew time is 11 p.m. and your son bowls home at 11.20 p.m. each Saturday night, you are right to point this out to him. But, let's face it, the curfew is pulling him home roughly on time – he is following the essence of what you have said – is it fair to ground him because of those twenty minutes? Is it really worth the hassle? It is maddening but he is obeying the spirit of the law if not quite to the letter. After all, he is a teenager and, in his mind, it is important to show his independence by obeying, but not quite exactly.

- ***Be precise.*** Teenagers are devious and if there is a slight ambiguity in the rules, they will exploit it. Deviousness is the teenager's trump card, so leave no room for misinterpretation. If you have agreed to pick up your son from Sam's house at 10 p.m., do not be surprised if you get a call to collect him from somewhere else. If you contest this, he will say, 'But I did go to Sam's and then we decided to call on James. You

didn't say we couldn't go out. What's the problem?'
You have been warned.

- **Always confront open disobedience.** You can expect some loose interpretation of the rules and some sneaky twisting of your words, but direct disobedience should always be challenged. Reiterate the rule, emphasize that his behaviour is unacceptable, tell him that the rule stays in place, and then it is up to you whether you impose sanctions or punishments or not. However, you are better to have this confrontation in the cold light of day instead of at two in the morning when everyone is tired and overwrought.

    Realistically, there will always be the odd occasion when your son will disobey your rules. When faced with the choice of obeying a rule or missing out on the fun with friends, the lure of the friends will win out every time, regardless of the consequences. Although you must challenge this behaviour, unless you are extremely lucky, be aware that rules will occasionally be broken.

Becoming streetwise

Part of a parent's greatest fear about letting their adolescent son out into society at large without their physical protection is the danger from street violence. And, sadly, this is a very real fear because street crime is on the increase. The Metropolitan Police figures show that of all street robberies, the proportion committed against under-eighteens rose from 35.1 per cent in 1999 to 40.3 per cent in 2001. The majority of these crimes are against

> I saw a guy getting picked on for so long that I spoke out. I got taken down but it's important to stand up for the guy. *Twenty-year-old*

boys and the rise in the number of attacks is greatest in inner cities.

It makes chilling reading for the parents of young boys. You fear that it only takes one ill-chosen glib or cocky comment on the part of your son to get him into serious trouble. More worrying still, very often attacks against boys happen in broad daylight, often on the way to or from home and school, and are completely unprovoked.

One of the most dangerous legacies of keeping our children cocooned at home and ferrying them everywhere by car is that many of them are unable to read the signs of impending trouble. They are also unaware of ways to avoid drawing attention to themselves. Coaching your son to be more streetwise can be a useful preventative measure against the chances of him becoming a victim.

What you can do
Obtain an information pack for your son from the Suzy Lamplugh Trust (tel: 020 8392 1839). They offer a comprehensive collection of personal safety advice for all sorts of different eventualities. Here are some useful extracts:

Preventing attack
Every time your son goes out, get him to ask himself the following questions:

- Where am I going?
- How am I getting there?
- How am I getting back?
- Am I prepared for changes of plan?
- Have I let people know where I am?

This is the first step to being safe because he is now aware of his own safety and any possible danger. Encourage him to let you (or someone) know if he changes his mind about any plans, even if he thinks you may not approve.

Do not make yourself a target
- Always let someone know where you are, especially if plans change.
- Always trust your instincts – if you have a 'funny feeling' about someone or something, do not ignore it, act on it.
- Remember drugs and alcohol dull your reflexes and reduce your awareness of danger.
- Have your keys ready so that you can get in the house quickly.
- Always remember, your voice is one of the best forms of defence.

When walking
- Never take a lift from a stranger – no matter how tired or cold you are.
- Avoid danger spots, like badly lit alleyways, subways or deserted car parks. Walk down the middle of the pavement if the street is deserted.

- Whenever possible, walk with a friend or stay near a group of people.
- Avoid passing stationary cars with their engines running and people sitting in them.
- Try to keep both hands free and do not walk with your hands in your pockets; get some gloves.
- Always take the route you know best and stick to well-lit, busy roads.
- Look confident – bullies tend to choose victims who look like an easy target – but do not look 'stuck up'.
- Walk facing on-coming traffic to avoid kerb crawlers.
- Try to keep your mind on your surroundings – with personal CD-players and radios you cannot hear trouble approaching.
- Make sure you have either a mobile (out of sight), phonecard, BT Chargecard or some spare change to make a phone call.

If your son feels threatened, impress the following on him:

- Get away from the threatening situation – run if necessary and do not attempt to fight back unless you really have to.
- If you think you are being followed, keep moving towards the nearest public place, crossing and recrossing the road – as soon as you get to the public place, phone either home or the police.
- If a vehicle pulls up next to you, turn and walk in the opposite direction – you can turn faster than a car –

again make for the nearest public place and use the phone.

On buses and trains

- Always wait for a bus or train in a well-lit place near other people if possible.
- On buses and trains, always try to sit near the driver or guard or in a busy carriage.
- Take notice of where the emergency alarms are and try to sit near them.
- Have your pass or correct change in your hand so that your wallet is out of sight.
- Carry extra money in case you get stranded and need to take another bus or train or ring for a lift.
- Ask someone to meet you if you are going to be alone at night when you get off at the bus stop or train station.

■ PROBLEM SOLVING
If your son is confronted or attacked, there are rules he should always follow

- If you can, get away from the situation – only fight if you really have to: someone is bound to end up getting hurt and it will probably be you.
- Try not to panic, breathe slowly and think clearly about how to react.
- Make as much noise as possible – yell at the top of your voice, giving a specific instruction like 'phone the police'.
- Always give away your wallet or phone rather than fighting – they can be replaced, you cannot.

Remember to keep your keys and your phone card/ change in your pocket.

- Get to a phone and call 999 (all calls are free, even on BT payphones). The operator will ask for name, address, emergency location and which emergency service you require – give the information as clearly as you can and ask for the police.
- After you have contacted the emergency services, call home and let them know where you are.

■ PROBLEM SOLVING
My son has been mugged

Victim Support in the UK explain that children often feel humiliated and guilty at having allowed themselves to be a victim, going over and over in their heads ways in which they might have avoided it happening. If they have lost something valuable in the attack, such as a phone or money, they may fear getting into trouble, and are reluctant to tell parents. An attack can shake their innocence as, for the first time, they realize that their familiar surroundings are not necessarily safe.

If your son is attacked, his first reaction is likely to be shock accompanied by an adrenaline rush. Do not be surprised if he does not rush home to tell you or does not

It's a real shock to discover how aggressive some people can get. That's where women are particularly helpful because they don't have that same kind of anger. If you mix with blokes all the time, they just reinforce the aggression. *Nineteen-year-old* burst into tears – that comes later. Initially, everything is confused and he may want to be on his own or to be quiet and contemplative for a while. This is no reflection on you or your relationship with your son – it is simply a natural, shock reaction.

> **Fighting**
> At the onset of adolescence, there is an upswing in competitive posturing. It is at about this time that boys feel the need to fight to prove who is tougher. Indeed, they talk a great deal about who is going to fight who but, in reality, there is only the occasional real fight. Expect lots of talk about how 'so-and-so is going to beat up such-and-such because he's a plonker' and how 'such-a-body could thrash this lad because he's a pussy', which may well make your toes curl but, thankfully, it rarely amounts to more than bravado and out-and-out fighting is rare.
>
> As your son passes through secondary school, fighting becomes less and less admired until, at around Year 10, it is considered a bit of a joke to fight because it's more important to be cool than to be tough. However, the one exception is when boys are drunk – then it is not only acceptable but half-expected.

Children who are victims of crime sometimes feel shock, anger, a desire for revenge, fear of going out alone, or fear of returning to the place where the attack occurred, such as school.

Over the coming days or even weeks after the attack, your son may develop symptoms, such as:

- Clinginess.
- Fear of going out on his own.
- Becoming withdrawn.
- Inability to sleep.
- Headaches.
- Stomach aches.
- Dropping off in schoolwork.

These are natural reactions which should pass. If these symptoms persist for several months or seem out of proportion to what happened, you should seek help.

What you can do
- **Gently encourage your son to talk about what happened.** Remember, boys in particular may be reluctant to talk because being a victim is inextricably linked with their understanding of their own masculinity and machismo. If he is reticent, he may find it easier to draw pictures or write a story about what happened.
- **Reassure him.** If he opens up, let him know that you are glad he has told you. Make it clear that you are concerned about his safety and not, for example, the loss of his mobile phone.
- **Try to make him feel secure.** Ask him what would make him feel safer – he might suggest something

you have not thought of. Let him know that you feel sorry and angry that he has had to suffer.

- **Allow him to say how he feels.** Give truthful answers to his questions and provide as much information as possible. If he wants to keep talking about what has happened, let him.
- **Be careful not to show your own fear and upset too much.** Boys are good at feeling that they must protect their parents from hurt.
- **Do not criticize his misjudgement.** Even if you believe that your son was taking an unnecessary risk, breaking a rule or being careless, this does not mean that he was inviting an assault. Kids do these things all the time and only rarely become the victims of crimes. *You must accept that the incident has happened.* The incident will have an impact and you cannot make everything all right again.
- **Encourage your son to return to his previous routines or habits.** This may help to overcome any fears slowly and in stages.
- **Give as much comfort as possible.** He may want more cuddles and physical comfort, but do not force it on him if that is not how you normally behave.
- **Try to stay close for a while.** Give him the comfort of your quiet physical presence.
- **Do you report an attack to the police?** This is a difficult call for a parent to make. Consult your son before going to the authorities – if he knows the boys concerned or they know where he lives, he may be fearful of reprisals.

- ***Remember, he will get over an attack.*** Although there will be after-effects, his natural confidence and trust in the world will re-emerge.
- *Contact* the Victim Support helpline (tel: 0845 3030 900 or visit www.victimsupport.org.uk).

■ CASE STUDY – Carolyn Carter's story

An unprovoked attack against your son is every parent's worst nightmare. That is precisely what happened to Carolyn's six-teen-year-old son and the family are still coming to terms with the long-term effects of the attack.

'Richard was walking alongside Bromley-by-Bow station in London with two male friends at 7.50 p.m. on 16 December. He was sixteen years old, 6 feet (1.8m) tall and well built. The three of them, two of whom were white and one was mixed race, were approached by four Asian youths who said, "Don't move. If you move, you'll get hit." An iron bar was produced from the sleeve of a jacket and Richard and his friends all ran.

'Richard was tripped up by the iron bar. More youths jumped from behind parked cars and behind walls. Eyewitnesses said there were approximately twenty of them. Richard was then beaten with the iron bar. A pizza delivery man and residents in the nearby flats obviously heard the commotion, and stopped the assault. The youths ran off.

'Police and an ambulance were called, and a lady held Richard's head in her arms until the ambulance arrived. I have never been able to trace those people to thank them which upsets me. He was taken to hospital by ambulance.

'The police came to my house at 10.30 p.m. I was out at a Christmas evening meal and my elder son took the message.

He phoned my mum and she came round, and rang the hospital not knowing whether Richard was dead or alive or what state he was in. She was told he had a head injury. My older son went straight to the hospital and, when I got in half an hour later, I heard the news. I just went straight there. Thank goodness I had not been drinking.

'When I saw Richard, he was sitting in a wheelchair covered in blood with his arm in a sling about to go to the X-ray department. I tried to be calm about it in front of him. I made some joke about the lengths a son will go to in order to muck up a mother's evening out. Once he had gone into X-ray, I lost it completely but at least he didn't see that. He was gone forty minutes, so I was able to compose myself. I then sent my older son home.

'Richard had a fractured shoulder blade, severe bruising to the neck and behind the ears. The beating to his head was so violent that he had a blood clot on his ear drum and he couldn't hear for a month. He still has impaired hearing. He had cuts and bruises on his fingers and wrists, and a head wound which required fifteen stitches and glue.

'We finally left the hospital at 3.15 a.m. after his treatment. He was on a high when I first arrived because the nurses had given him some pain relief, but as we walked away from the hospital, he totally broke down and sobbed. He wanted to know why him. He referred to the fact that he'd already lost his dad (I was widowed seven years earlier), and he was angry because he hadn't done anything. A police officer later told us that Richard was the victim of an unprovoked racial attack.

'We had to make return visits to the hospital to attend the fracture clinic, and he still sees the Ear, Nose and Throat consultant regularly. He also had to have a brain scan.

'A few days after the attack, we had the good fortune that Victim Support came to visit us (the police must have sent them I suppose). A young girl not much older than Richard came to see him. She was Asian and I thought at first that he might not see her. Anyway, she spent a lot of time with Richard. It was invaluable to me. I did what I could but it was difficult. He would get so far with me and then clam up. If he got emotional, then I'd get upset.

'I went through a phase of being very angry. I also went through feelings of guilt because I had asked him not to go to that area but it was early evening, after all. I spoke to Victim Support and they were helpful to me too. My older son was also extremely angry. I was almost as worried about what he might try to do as I was about the state that Richard was in. It took him well over a week to calm down, he was so upset. An assault has a knock-on effect because all the family was badly affected. My parents and mother-in-law were upset that someone they love had been hurt.

'After the attack, I was anxious every time Richard went out. I would have loved to have kept him in but I couldn't do that – but he wouldn't go out alone. I suppose it was a help to know that he was always in the company of others.

'Richard had to go with the police to show them where it had happened. Then he and I spent several hours in a police station making a statement but I knew they would never get them because they didn't have any CCTV evidence.

'I couldn't get Richard to go outside the door for over a week. He was too frightened. Also, he had had his head partly shaved and there was dried blood in his hair because he wasn't allowed to wash it until the stitches came out. He was embarrassed. He wore a cap inside and outside the house, and only took it off to sleep.

'One of the hardest things is that Richard kept asking "Why me?" and I couldn't answer him. He was in that place for the first time having gone to meet a friend who was painting his uncle's flat. It makes you feel inadequate because you can't answer all of the questions that he asked.

'Three years on, I don't think he is fully over it. He has carried on with his life but he doesn't talk about it. Stacy, the Victim Support volunteer, keeps in touch by phone and he welcomes that. But he seems to feel as though he was at fault in some way. It's as if he's ashamed that it happened to him.

'On one occasion, we had to go through Bromley-by-Bow station on the underground train on the way to the hospital. Richard went as white as a sheet and shook like a leaf. I thought he was going to be sick. He won't go on that route any more and he'd rather go a longer route than go through that station again.

'I still have problems with him when we have to return to the hospital to see the consultant. He gets very stroppy and verbally quite aggressive. He is very uncomfortable and fidgety. He once said to me that every time he returns to the hospital he relives that night.'

Although Richard's attackers were never caught, Victim Support* processed the claim to the Criminal Injuries Compensation Board and Richard and his family have since received a payment.

---

* Victim Support Helpline – tel: 0845 3030 900

12

Recharging your batteries

Do you remember the permanent exhaustion of being a new parent? Somehow it's an accepted part of the new parent scene. But ten or fifteen years down the road, do you still expend energy on your son as if it were an inexhaustible supply. You may have relinquished the broken nights, but it is a straight swap for picking him up from parties at 2 a.m., and ferrying him to and from football training/tennis/guitar lessons (delete as applicable).

Effectively, there are probably more demands on your time now than ever and your son needs you emotionally too. Your son has a voracious appetite for life and new experiences, and since he is not fully self-reliant yet, you have to shore up his social life as well as trying to run your own (plus possibly running a home and a job). Where is it all going to end?

As a parent, you expect to make sacrifices of your time and your energy for the sake of your children – but this should only be up to a point. It is not healthy to run yourself into the ground for your son. Naturally, you want to help him and it is your duty to support him as much as you can, but you must be realistic. You may spend years stretching yourself too thin on his behalf, and yet your son will simply accept all your efforts as part of his birthright. He very likely takes you for granted and, just as summer follows spring, you end up feeling hurt and let down. It is just one small step to 'After all I've done for him' martyrdom.

Parents who stay at home complain of feeling over-domesticated and undervalued. They dislike being viewed as an extension of their partner or kids, and not as an individual in their own right. On the other hand, working parents moan about having the worst of both worlds (and not doing either very well), and they may have a faint trace of guilt. Whichever camp you fall into, your stewing resentment can lead to emotional (if not physical) exhaustion and deteriorating health. You have to remember that you can only maintain being overstretched for so long before you snap. If you are constantly feeling hard done by or overextended, you can no longer be an effective parent.

Perhaps if you look at how this perpetual state of tension affects you, you will gain a better understanding of why you react to your son as you do, and why parenting can seem like such a labour of love.

Why you respond that way
To get to the nub of your responses to your son, you have to take a good hard look at yourself, and be emotionally honest. Before you begin to panic, baring your soul is simply the first step to understanding why you react to your son as you do, and why your reactions vary so much.

What is happening in your own internal world affects how you interact with others, including your son. If you are unconsciously feeling put upon, then it is natural to be somewhat churlish towards the object of your resentment – among others, your son. More often than not, though, your general ennui, feelings that there should be more to life than this, plus an underlying irritability, make your reactions to your son so unpredictable. On a good day, you may respond benignly to his robust over-exuberance, but on a day when your underlying emotions are winding you up, you react with full volume and rhetoric. Do not forget either that your son's temperament, moods, and behaviour are always shifting too, so if you get the wrong combination on any given day, you can expect fireworks.

If you are aware of your emotional state, your responses to your son will take you less by surprise. However, if you refuse to acknowledge how you feel, then you will become increasingly tense and, under the slightest provocation, you will blow your top, and respond in ways you would really rather not.

Once conscious of your emotions, you can equip yourself with the necessary skills and tactics to moderate these explosive feelings when you experience them. This does not mean that you have to suppress your emotions. By all means, tell your son how you feel. In fact, warn him off if you feel a little testy. However, now you can spot more readily whether you are berating him because of his behaviour or if, in fact, you are mad at him because how you feel inside is rearing its ugly head (see Chapter Ten, page 230).

If your son sees you expressing how you feel, it gives him a better handle on people's strengths and weaknesses, and a more realistic view of life. He sees that his parent is not omnipotent (despite his constant criticism, the all-pervasive power of a parent is still a firmly held belief by many offspring), and this helps him to accept his own feelings and sense of self – warts and all. It should also help him to talk about his own emotions.

Go easy on yourself
It is very hard to talk or to be objective about your feelings if you are still angry, tired or resentful, so why not reevaluate your feelings? Give yourself a pat on the back for a job well done – you may not be the perfect parent but, if you are honest, you are not making such a bad job of things either. Why not give yourself the occasional reward for the parenting job you do? Incentive and reward schemes are successful in the workplace, so why not in the home?

You can also talk to other parents, particularly if they are more experienced. A 'Did you find that too?' conversation can be an invaluable way to boost flagging belief in your parenting skills, and an informal chat about what you are going through can often leave you with the heartening impression that perhaps you have not done so badly after all.

Another reason why you might be overcritical and snappy with your son is because you remember your own childhood, and make the inevitable comparisons. This is a fruitless and unhealthy exercise, but it is something we all do. How many times have you found yourself thinking, 'I'd never have spoken to my dad like that' or reflected wistfully that when your mother said 'No,' it meant 'No'?

And that is the crux of the matter – any comparison gives you an uneasy feeling that you are not quite in control, and that you are not the parent you should be. It does not help matters that your own parents are still alive and a constant reminder that you have been weighed, measured, and found wanting in the parenting department. Yet direct comparisons between your childhood and your son's behaviour now are completely invalid. Life for today's young people is completely different. You have not failed just because your son does not instantly obey – after all, you have encouraged him to speak up for himself and to be open.

Parents everywhere would feel much better if it were publicly acknowledged that it is actually harder to get children today to comply and, in large measure, that is because the social boundaries that existed a generation ago have gone. And to be frank, it is too soon to say whether we have got it right or whether our parents have got good cause to chunter. The proof of the pudding, as it were, is in the adults our children turn into and there are good grounds to be optimistic.

Invest in yourself

Sometimes it is important to put yourself first. Your son's needs do not always have to take primacy (and that goes for the whole family, incidentally). It is okay to refuse one of your son's requests on the grounds that you have something more pressing to do for yourself. Or it may be that you simply do not want to do him a favour because he has been so obnoxious to you recently. In which case, tell him so.

He may not like it, but he will survive. Be prepared for a tirade of invective about being the worst parent in the world or mutterings under his breath. Nonetheless, with a prevailing wind and a dash of luck, he may just realize, on quiet reflection, that you're not a doormat and that you too have feelings.

Enjoy your son

How often do you hear someone say that they really enjoy being a parent? Or that they enjoy their children? If pushed, a tipsy parent might admit to being proud of their boy, but enjoying his company? It is far more common to hear parents discussing their concerns about Daniel's grades or James' lack of football prowess. Where has all the pleasure gone?

Since you have invested so much time in your son, you might as well start enjoying him. After all, there are no guarantees that you will reap the rewards of good service when your eighteen years are up. He could be off without a backwards glance.

The big problem may be that when you do get to spend time with your son, you are so preoccupied with what you could or should be doing, you do not relax and enjoy the moment. If you give yourself up to it rather than worrying about whether you've got enough leave left for Christmas or when you'll get a chance to do the shopping, then you and your son will have a good time. Throw yourself unreservedly into having fun and spending time with your son while you can, and just enjoy sharing his experiences. Despite the current climate of parents fretting over trivia, there is no shame in admitting that you enjoy your son. Make the most of him while he is still with you.

Whether or not he gets the point, you are doing the right thing. If you do too much for your son, this breeds dependence at a time when you should be fostering self-reliance in him. It is important to learn how to say 'No'. Once you have grown accustomed to the principle of putting yourself first now and again, you will find this notion has an uncanny way of creeping into other areas of your life. Before you know it, you will be telling the head-mistress that you cannot help at the summer fête because of other commitments.

Make time for yourself
At home parents have to get away from the idea that parenting is a role of self-sacrificing servitude. To offer your family the best of yourself, you have to look after yourself. Do not view time for relaxation or doing something for you as an indulgence. Rather, see it as an investment for your family. This is not just a thinly veiled stab at justification for being selfish; it is a fact. If you do what makes you feel good or fulfilled, then you will feel better in yourself, have greater self-esteem, and a healthier zest for life. And this can only be a good thing for the whole family. Only a fool could miss the point that everyone benefits from this scenario. And try to include a bit of pampering or relaxation time too – to quote a well-known cosmetic advertising slogan, 'Because you're worth it'.

> Most of the time society views me as either Nathan's mum or Pete's wife. The only time I feel like a person in my own right is once a week at my French conversation class.   *Thirty-nine-year-old, mother of two*

> Being in a reading group has been my salvation. If I didn't have it, I think I'd go insane.
> *Forty-two-year-old, mother of three*

Now, before you throw up your hands in protest, we can all say, 'But I just don't have the time.' It is true that for most parents, there simply are not enough hours in the day. However, it's a case of prioritizing and something has to give. Time for you is important and if it means that some chore does not get done or that you have to enlist the help of family and friends (which you can repay in kind), then so be it.

What you can do
You know better than anyone what it is that gives you the greatest pleasure or the best sense of fulfilment. You will almost certainly have your own ideas for ways to indulge yourself and to relax. However, here are a few suggestions garnered from other parents to achieve that bit of extra time:

- ***Find a babysitter.*** If you cannot pay a reliable teenager or neighbour, find some like-minded friends and set up a babysitting service.
- ***Use babysitters for 'self-time'.*** Rather than just for work or social engagements with partner and friends.
- ***Do not try to pack domestic chores into your few free hours.*** Instead of food shopping, for example, have a massage and order on-line from a supermarket home delivery service that night.

- **Relax your standards.** Sounds louche, doesn't it? But your house does not have to be spotless the whole time. If it means getting to your evening class, you can turn a blind eye to a bit of a mess, surely. There is always time to tidy up before visitors arrive.

- **Have a sacred space or part of the day.** Have time where your kids do not disturb you and where you can relax temporarily. Even if it is just a corner of your bedroom for five or ten minutes, get into the habit of making that space or that time sacrosanct.

- **Commit to giving your son a certain amount of your time each day with your undivided attention.** This is his time and it should be important to you both – and far better than begrudgingly giving half your attention for what seems like hours and hours on end.

- **Make time to talk to your partner.** Between individual work and social commitments and ferrying kids to and fro, you can become ships that pass in the night. Set aside a little time each day to exchange news and to talk, preferably without the kids interfering.

- **Consciously relax.** Sometimes you may catch yourself on the way to work or while doing some chore, and your shoulders are up around your ears. Make an effort to learn a breathing or relaxation technique and employ it regularly throughout the day.

- **Occasionally eat out en famille in a good restaurant.** It may be simpler to buy your son fast food and eat on the hoof, but occasionally take pleasure in eating good food together as a family in a 'proper' restaurant, and talk as you dine.

- **Spend time with other families that you like.** If there are parents whose company you enjoy, organize social activities together. Even if the children are not especially close, they will muddle along and you can all enjoy a barbecue or outing as relaxation time.

■ PROBLEM SOLVING
I can't cope any more

Sometimes, a combination of unfortunate life events, such as the death or illness of a loved one, a separation or divorce, or maybe a house move away from family and friends, can bring overwhelming pressure that makes you feel that you simply cannot cope. For others, it is the sheer relentlessness of being a parent or the strain of a particularly demanding member of the family that takes its toll, and leaves you feeling like burrowing under the duvet and never coming out.

You almost certainly know the importance of good food and exercise, and looking after yourself in times of stress, but here are some other steps you can take when you feel like you cannot go on:

- **Pay a visit to your doctor.** However, avoid pill-popping if at all possible. If a specific situation has caused your panic and anxiety, bear in mind that antidepressants may take weeks or months to work. Conversely, if it is the mundane that is causing the problems, sleeping pills and tranquillizers may leave you too knocked out to deal with the kids.
- **Head for counselling.** A psychotherapist can work as a neutral pressure valve when the going is rough. If your problems are seated in family life, a family

therapist may be the answer. Find a qualified counsellor in your area: www.bacp.co.uk

- *Give yourself a mental and emotional break.* Go away for the weekend. Go on a course or visit friends who make you feel more positive – either on your own if you can wangle it or with the family. When you remove yourself physically and/or emotionally from the problem, it is easier to be objective.

- *Use positive affirmations or mantras.* Keep saying to yourself out loud, 'I am a strong person and I can cope.' Choose something that resonates with you and does not make you feel uncomfortable. The Buddhist mantra, 'Om tare tuttare ture svaha' is the mantra of Green Tara, who was born from the tears of the Buddha of compassion. If you chant this mantra when you feel down, it is said to help concentrate the mind, and draw positive energy to the person who chants it.

- *Learn a relaxation technique.* Yoga, meditation, tai chi, breathing exercises – whatever appeals – they are all great ways to help you deal with stress, and to encourage relaxation.

- *Go easy on yourself.* Do not attempt to give up smoking/caffeine/chocolate, etc. or to go on a fast or diet while feeling low. A few more days or weeks is not going to make one iota of difference, and why make things harder by ditching props at such a difficult time.

- *Turn to your friends and loved ones for support.* And not just for practical help. If you feel miserable, a hug from a friend or loved one is now scientifically proven to do good. In particular, physical contact such as hugging, stroking or cuddling produces

> Sometimes there is so much going on that I feel like my life is out of control. It gives me a panicky, trapped feeling. I don't want every hour of every day planned out. Nothing is spontaneous any more.
>
> *Thirty-eight-year-old, mother of two*

stress-lowering hormones called oxytocins in women (remarkably this does not apply for men). Even if a woman does not particularly like physical contact, tests show that being held or touched by friends will still make her body produce the oxytocin because it is a hard-wired biological response.

Remember you are a couple

Sometimes it is hard to believe there was life BC (Before Children), and your days as a couple seem a distant and rather blurry memory. However, your partnership is a very important component of your family life and it needs nurturing.

If you have always put yourself far down the list of priorities, it is a fairly safe bet that, in your mind's eye, your relationship is also languishing somewhere in the middle rankings. Yet it is important that you take care of your relationship and build in some time for the two of you.

Without doubt, we all lead hectic and stressed lives, and you may spend a good deal of your time running on your emotional and physical reserves. Nevertheless, just because it is not always easy, there is no real excuse for the destructive spiral that affects many parent couples. Unfortunately, at the end of a long day, as soon as you greet each other, it becomes a competition to see who is the most stressed, and who has had the worst day. Each partner raises the misery stakes and each of you ends up feeling resentful, misunderstood, and miserable.

You may have to take a leap of faith on this one but in order to break the cycle of negative one-upmanship, why not focus solely on the good news when you exchange stories about your day? Try it for a few days and see what happens. Once you both realize that it is not a competition to see who is the best burning martyr, you will start to enjoy each other more, or at least resent each other less.

Make an effort to build in some time for you as a couple. It is good to feel great about your partner again. If you spend a little more time alone together, it may come as some surprise to learn that not only are you pretty decent company but that your partner still finds you very attractive. Injecting some space and time for each other into your hectic lives does not necessarily have to lead to rekindled romance, if that is not to your taste. However, it is good to rediscover an interest in the real person lurking behind the familiar role of parent/partner/chauffeur. If you can remain happy and excited by your partner's company, you stand a far better chance of avoiding the oft-quoted trap of having to reacquaint yourself with a near stranger when the kids eventually fly the nest.

Getting it right

It may seem like a pipe dream to fit all this time for yourself, your relationship, and one-to-one time with your son into an already over-stuffed schedule, but it is possible if you really want to. When you realize that if you are more fulfilled and relaxed, it is much easier to be a better parent and to enjoy your son, it starts to make sense. It is like

> Just going out for a meal on our own once in a while gives us a chance to catch up. Once we've discussed all the practical issues that need sorting out, we've got time for us as individuals again. It's very important.
>
> *Peter, father of two*

going to the gym – you immediately feel the good effects and wonder why you did not do it sooner – and then you slip back into your old ways. It is the same with investing in yourself – you will feel much better and your whole family will reap the rewards. Nonetheless, when some additional pressures crop up and you sacrifice your time for yourself just this week, before you know it, a month has gone by and you are back to feeling ratty and hard done by. Actually it does not matter if you lapse, that is real life – we all have periods when making extra time for yourself would just be one more source of stress – but once the pressure is off, make a concerted effort to return to your self-promoting ways. It pays dividends.

Like so many things, good parenting largely comes down to a positive frame of mind. You have to view being a parent as something you are doing for yourself. If you go into it with the expectation of a return or as some sort of investment in your future, you are missing the point. The Eastern philosophies maintain that if you give unconditionally, you get back what you give out, and more. This principle is never more apt than when applied to parenting.

You were full of optimism and excitement when you chose to become a parent and, despite the odd inevitable hiccup along the way, if you can maintain this positive approach to your parenting role, you will greatly increase the chances of family life being fulfilling and enjoyable – not just for you but for your son too.

■ CASE STUDY – Annie's story

It is important to keep an element of your life that is fulfilling and special to you. It can keep you sane at difficult times, as Annie explains.

'I started studying to become an astrologer in 1981 and Luke was born in 1983. So, I was already on a path before I had children. It took me a little longer to qualify than I had thought it would because of the kids, but I was committed to it.

'Even though I loved every aspect of motherhood, having something else in my life that was also all-consuming was very important. It was my space and I connected with that whole other side of myself. It lies dormant with very young children but it was always in the background. I had a lot of people around me that I could talk that language to, and this helped to keep it alive.

'I really enjoyed being a mum to young children and I didn't wish they were out of the way to give me more time to study. Having something else that fulfilled me gave me the energy to do both.

'Because Francis and I separated quite early on, he would take the boys off for the weekend occasionally. It was lovely to have that time to myself and then it was lovely to have them back. That was the upside of being a single parent.

'It made me realize that for me to be a good mum, it was essential to do something that I wanted to do for me. As wholehearted as I was as a mother, without that other side of my life being fulfilled, I would not have been as conscious of all that there was that I enjoyed in being a parent.

'Despite the pressures, it was important to me that I kept my interests going. I used to study when they were in bed. It was impossible to do it with them around. I kept the kids and my astrology separate. It kept me sane.

'Luke has grown up with me being an astrologer and having meditation groups in the house etc. He is respectful of it, if a bit sceptical. He knows me as a working mum and I don't think he ever felt like my work or interests impinged on his time.

'At nineteen, he is now completely independent. If I had tried to live my life through him, I would have been in a sorry, baleful state because he is now so independent. As he has grown up, that extra dimension to my life has filled a space more and more. He still needs me in some ways, of course, but it would have been harder to let him go if I didn't have my other interests. I would have leaned more heavily on him.

'As a single parent, it can be more of a temptation to put everything into a child. Of course, there are lots of things factored in like your temperament and circumstances, etc. but, after the death of my younger son and Francis had gone to Canada, it was just Luke and me. We were a very close unit and, for a while, my emotional needs were met by Luke because we had a loving relationship. I could see how, had I not been a certain type of person, it could have been emotionally insular. It's easy to invest all of your emotional needs in your child and to expect them to meet those needs. It's imperative that you have outside interests and be aware that it's a parent-child relationship, and not to lean on him as if it's an adult relationship. For me, the boundaries were never blurred, but I was aware that I got a lot of comfort from the relationship. Not just as a single parent but also as a bereaved parent.

'I don't feel, looking at him now, as if he carries that. Luke doesn't feel responsible for me or for my happiness. He is naturally self-reliant. Rather than cloister him, I have given him a lot of freedom, and having my own life and interests allowed me to do that.'

Troubleshooting

Fridge clearers

Q: I have three boys who eat me out of house and home. A box of Mr Kipling's cakes lasts about two minutes and then they are hungry again. I cannot keep pace with them. How can I fill them up and yet avoid resorting to junk foods?

A: Cheryl, mother of two. The key is to give them large portions of carbohydrates to fill them up. Bread is the best thing. Enormous quantities of toast etc.! I think this is certainly important as they get older and do burn up large quantities of energy.

A: Carole, mother of two boys. I find it is better to cut fruit up into pieces for them to eat when they get home from school. They need food that is no effort to eat. Also good for after school are toast, crackers or cheese. Kids will eat relatively healthily if pre-prepared, but not if they have to peel or chop themselves. Too much effort!

Another of my strategies when they come in saying 'I'm hungry, what can I have?' and what they really mean is 'I want a biscuit', is to say they can have some fruit first and then a biscuit.

A: Dinah, mother of three. I always bulk buy and I always bulk cook. If I cook a meal, I make sure I have got loads of left-overs for the next day for snacks. I batch bake and batch freeze and I shop at Macro.

A: Linda, mother of one. After school is the prime 'fill up' time … as well as any times of boredom! The key target is the fridge … then the cupboards. So, my best option as a vegetarian mother is to cut seasonal fruits – strawberries, melon, apple, pear – and place them in an appetizing promi- nent position in the fridge to meet the initial onslaught. For the subsequent onslaught, cheese and tomato sandwiches, cucumber pieces, and food that takes some time to munch! Nice fresh bread still remains a good filler for my son. An alternative would be to lock up all food avenues or have noth- ing tasty available!

What the experts say
A: Psychiatrist. Be clear about what the kids can and cannot eat. Teach them about healthy eating. Get them interested in cooking and nutrition, if possible. It's important for kids to understand not to raid the fridge of things that are being saved for special occasions etc., and that mum doesn't get frazzled from cooking all the time.

A: Agony Aunt. Most kids won't bother to try and cook any- thing – it has to be instant. Try keeping a bowl of filling soup in the fridge that they can dip into, or perhaps a big bowl of pasta salad laced with salami and tasty morsels. Keep plenty of bread in the house – it has to be sliced, most kids can't cut ordinary bread. Much as I hate it, most teenagers love to snack on bowls of cereal, so try and cut down the sugar and salt by buying cornflakes or plainer cereal. Buy a toasted sandwich maker (don't expect it to get cleaned) and plenty of cheese. Also make sure you've got a robust toaster and a self-shutting fridge.

Get used to the idea that you can't fill them up. Unfortunately, their eating habits have been established by the time they are ten so it's no good suddenly suggesting they eat loads of fruit or whatever when they've not shown any interest in the past. Acquire a cash and carry card if possible (or try and marry into the Sainsbury family!).

Pocket money
Q: I have always resisted giving my son pocket money but realize it is inevitable one day. So when is a good age to start, what is a reasonable amount and what should I expect it to cover?

A: Sarah, mother of two. When I was young, we used to go to the shops with our friends and spend our money together. We were very aware of how much everybody got. My sons probably haven't got a clue what their friends get because they never go shopping with them.

A: Cheryl, mother of two. I don't give pocket money at all. I don't feel it is necessary. They can earn extra money by doing jobs around the house, and the money they get given from relatives at birthdays and Christmas means they don't really need pocket money these days.

A: Clare, mother of two. My sons are very naive about money. They have no idea about how it is come by so I try to instil in them that it is not inexhaustible. If Robert is short of a certain amount to buy a Gameboy game I won't give him the balance. He has to wait until he has got next week's pocket money to get what he wants.

A: John, father of three. I provide what the kids want as treats in return for good behaviour or results. This works better than pocket money.

A: Heather, mother of three. They get pocket money when they begin to understand prices and change. They only get enough for basics, i.e. comics, sweets, etc. when little – it increases with each birthday. They also have the opportunity to earn more by doing jobs around the house, setting the table, emptying bins, babysitting when they get older!

What the experts say
A: Psychiatrist. Each family has to feel confident about doing it their own way. Principles about the value of money and teaching them how to save and spend wisely are important. You can teach them to delay gratification and plan for what they really want in life by letting them earn money for tasks accomplished, which builds self-esteem, and builds up sums towards getting certain purchases. Money can be used as a reward within a behavioural plan as well. Money at a pre-agreed rate given after the event as payment for work done tends to work better than when given as a bribe where the money is given before, and bartering happens in which the parent is not in control. Money can be a great incentive to make us all productive with our time,

although it mustn't substitute the sense of accomplishment we get from a job well done, and from being of service.

You need a system to make it happen the way you want it to happen. It's best to work out a system that fits with your family beliefs and is in keeping with the culture around you, rather than leaving it to random chance.

A: Agony Aunt. Whatever rate of pocket money you suggest, it will always be half what other kids get, according to your son. So ring around 'tame' parents and get the low-down. Decide whether you're giving pocket money and providing all clothes etc. or an allowance. If you opt for the latter, then draw up a clear list of what you think it should cover, and discuss it with your son. Does it include haircuts, out of school clothes, for example? You may feel it's better for you to buy all items to do with schooling – clothes, bus fares, books, school shoes, etc. – and leave the allowance to be spent on what he wants to spend it on.

My son is a quitter
Q: We have always encouraged our son to try different activities but he does not stick at any of them. He's tried the guitar and the piano. He had tennis, karate and ju jitsu lessons, and although he starts with great enthusiasm, after a while, he seems to lose interest and wants to give it up – usually after we've bought him all the gear. What should we do?

A: Cheryl, mother of two. You have to make it clear that they must practise or they won't be allowed to do it. I use a timer to make sure that Rowan does his practising! I also make him do it just before *The Simpsons* with the threat that he won't be allowed to watch it if he doesn't.

A: Carole, mother of two. My boys earn 10p for each day's practising they do, which they can then spend in the sweet shop on Saturday. This worked quite well for a while!

A: Dinah, mother of three. I don't buy any gear until he has committed, with the understanding that he has to keep doing it once I have paid for the gear. He is not allowed it until he has gone regularly for so many weeks.

What the experts say
A: Psychiatrist. It helps to make sure that your son is well motivated from the start, rather than acting on a whim. By helping think through all the pros and cons of taking up the hobby before starting, he can make an active choice if he still feels keen once the cons are fully explored. The commitment is about agreeing the deal – what you and he will and will not do, in advance, so that you both know the rules.

The principles of behavioural theory are helpful here. For children to grow up with a sense of responsibility, they have to learn that there are consequences to their actions. You have to set expectations for your children and explain the consequences of their actions. 'If you don't practise, then I won't pay for lessons any more and you will no longer be allowed to have lessons.' Then it's his decision. But you have to mean what you say and be prepared to stop the lessons.

A: Agony Aunt. Write it off to experience. You can't make him stick at it. In the right circumstances, you can borrow equipment, but this is not usually the case because hand-me-down instruments or equipment are often a bit worn and don't do much to encourage the player. Liaise with the school/teacher and if your son has real promise or is very keen, you have to take the plunge and buy the instrument. You can often buy second-hand and sell it on if and when he finishes with it.

Term time breaks

Q: We've got access to my in-laws' timeshare villa in the Algarve, but it would mean taking our son out of school to go. The school policy discourages holidays in term time and we have to get written permission from the headmistress. Can we justify taking him out for a cheap holiday?

A: Linda, mother of one. I try to avoid any development of tummy ache/unfounded illness breaks but am happy to enable travel breaks. These are usually at the end of term when activities at school are very light or superficial. Travel is one of the greatest teachers to us in our home and we need the additional time to enable journeys, especially long distance. This outweighs any disadvantages, we believe.

A: Cheryl, mother of three. It very much depends on age. Obviously the older they get the more important it is not to take them out.

A: Heather, mother of three. Term time breaks should not be encouraged; however, I feel that holidays themselves can be educational, i.e. geography, languages, foreign food, and currency, cultural, and religious issues.

A: Carole, mother of two. I think as they get thirteen weeks a year off school, one ought to be able to organize one's holidays within that time and I really don't approve of people taking them out for a whole fortnight just so they can get a cheaper deal. If one is going to take them out of school, then try and do it towards the end of term or around half-term breaks. Never let them miss school at the start of term. This is an important time when groups, timetables, etc. are set and they will miss a lot if they are not there.

However, the odd days for weekends or whatever are not too critical and should be allowed.

A: Peter, father of four. It's a disgrace that holiday companies and airlines hike prices up so much during school holidays. We can only afford to take our four abroad in term time.

What the experts say
A: Psychiatrist. Children have particular needs at different developmental stages. A decision has to be dependent on the child's age, your family situation, finances, and your attitude to academia. All these things have to be put in a decisional balance to see what is best for everyone.

A: Agony Aunt. Generally I'm against taking kids out of school. I know travel is a vital element of a child's education and is a great confidence booster, but it is disruptive to take them out during term time. They do miss vital elements of their education, and I feel that school holidays are so long these days that it doesn't take much effort to plan a holiday to fit in with them. My only exception to this rule would be if there is a once in a lifetime trip – say to Australia or a special long-haul, where the education of seeing different countries would compensate – but even then I wouldn't do it over the age of fourteen.

Alcohol

Q: My fourteen-year-old son and his friends have shared the odd can of beer, bought for them by an older brother. Should I turn a blind eye or clamp down on this under-age drinking?

A: Heather, mother of three. We allow them to taste it, but don't make an issue of it. We also point out homeless alcoholics on trips to the city.

A: Pam, mother of two. You tend to turn a blind eye. Our David got horrendously drunk on cider at fourteen but it was a long time before we found out. His brother looked after him. It wasn't really a problem for our boys because they were always too keen on their sport.

A: Peter, father of four. I'd rather Michael started drinking under my supervision than furtively with his mates. I'd prefer it if he were a bit older, but realistically fourteen is quite common to start among our circle of friends.

What the experts say

A: Psychiatrist. Educate children fully about alcohol and its effects so that they learn how to use it wisely. Supervise them closely while they are learning. I would not leave a room of boys on their own with alcohol. It's about supervision and education. I would not ban it because they will do the opposite in that case.

A: Agony Aunt. I recommend an open, liberal attitude and would let him try a little at home. Whatever your attitude, they'll try it anyway at sometime and will all get horribly tipsy – it's part of growing up.

Allow a small glass of wine on high days and holidays (fourteen plus) – most kids hate it so it's not a worry. Beer is what boys do like – given the chance, thirteen- or fourteen-year-olds will endeavour to sneak beer – perhaps at a family barbecue where they are not monitored, for example. The rule should be one bottle each and then trouble if more is taken – but implementing it may be difficult!

Body Piercing and Tatoos
Q: My seventeen-year-old son wants an earring. I have put my foot down and said that he cannot have any piercing while he lives under my roof but he says as soon as he is eighteen, he's going to go and get it done. And I am worried that he might get more than just his ear pierced. What can I do?

A: Pam, mother of two. I prayed they wouldn't get drunk with their mates and come home with a tattoo. In fact, I think I said as much to them but I never actually forbade it.

A: Heather, mother of three. Body piercing is a phase – ignore it. There are worse things such as drugs or violence.

What the experts say
A: Psychiatrist. With adolescents you are usually better off going with the flow. By refusing permission you may well be asking for rebellion and a much more extreme outcome. Parents generally prefer to know what their adolescents are up to so that they can supervise what is done, even if they do not fully agree with it, when the alternative is extreme oppositional behaviour.

You can set limits on adolescents but you have to choose a few important limits rather than be over-restrictive on everything. The meaning of body piercing varies in different families and cultures, so the limits you set will depend on this.

As a parent there are some things that I would put my foot down over, but this is not one of them.

A: Agony Aunt. Body piercing, green hair, etc., it's usually just a phase and one that is part of an ancient tribal bonding – from Maori to Masai – it's gone on for centuries. Often kids do it to shock or rebel and there's little you can do, especially once he's eighteen. I know a number of kids that have had this done and within months have been bored of the look and let the holes grow over. If your child is still at school, you'll probably find that there will be rules about this which will preclude him from piercings – at least during term times.

Teenage sex under our roof

Q: I have been asked by our seventeen-year-old son and his sixteen-year-old girlfriend if they can sleep together at our house after a family wedding that we are all attending together in the summer. They have been together for about six months and I have a strong suspicion that they are already having sex but I have never had to confront it before. I do not really want to encourage this but neither do I want to seem prudish.

A: Heather, mother of three. Sex should be discussed openly from an early age and should be discouraged under your roof as it shows no respect for parents or younger children.

A: *Pam, mother of two*. I know it happens but I don't want them to expect that they can. I wouldn't expect them to ask. We've always been very open about sex but I would like them to respect my home.

What the experts say

A: *Psychiatrist*. The same principles apply as for body piercing. But this may be higher up the hierarchy of limit setting, and you may feel that your son has to respect the few important rules of your home of which this may be one, until such a point where they become more committed to each other.

If you do consent to this, however, although the girl is of the age of consent, her parents still have responsibility for her and it would be preferable to discuss this with them as the repercussions could be complicated. Some parents would feel fine and others would feel extremely uncomfortable, depending on their culture. It's a question of weighing up the pros and cons, and it's going to vary from family to family.

A: *Agony Aunt*. If his girlfriend is regular, then you have to accept that sex is going to happen, and better where you can have some parental influence. Having said that, I would feel strongly about the influence this would have on younger kids. It's a difficult one, this.

It's going to happen under your own roof without you knowing it at some point so you have to have an element of openness. I think you have to insist that your son and his girlfriend are very discreet if, after discussion with him, you feel his actions are appropriate.

Should I stay or should I go?

Q: We have agreed that our eighteen-year-old son can have a party at our house when his A levels are over. He wants us to go out for the evening but I am reluctant. What do you think?

A: Pam, mother of two. I would go but I would give them a time limit. Also I would buy the alcohol rather than let them bring their own.

A: Mike, father of three. There's no way I'd leave them alone in my house. I know what we got up to as teenagers and, hypocrite or not, I don't want it going on in my home.

A: Lisa, mother of two. We allowed our son to have a party in the house and we went out. The house was pretty wrecked with vomit in the bedrooms and all sorts. But it wasn't us who said, 'Never again,' it was our son! So, if he learnt a valuable lesson, perhaps it wasn't such a high price to pay after all.

What the experts say

A: Psychiatrist. I would probably stay unobtrusively. I would want to know what is going on in my house.

A: Agony Aunt. It's not always your child but other kids that cause the trouble. I recommend that you stay, but at a distance. Provide filling food – french bread and so on, and beer but no spirits. Most of the party-goers will bring in their own drink, including spirits, so it is hard to police. Why not have a barbecue in the garden so that there is less chance of accidents happening in the home?

Saturday or part-time jobs

Q: Michael is sixteen and he wants to take a part-time job at a local fast food outlet to save up some money. However, he is studying hard for GCSEs. Should I allow this?

A: Heather, mother of three. I think children working at part-time jobs should be encouraged. It teaches them time management.

A: Pam, mother of two. As long as it doesn't interfere with his schooling, it's good for him to earn a bit of money if he can. He can learn the value of money that way.

What the experts say

A: Psychiatrist. It depends so much on the son. If he is academically bright but he is low on self-confidence, the job could be good for him. It could take his focus away from exams and build his confidence so that he realizes that academia is not the be all and end all.

However, if he was the sort of boy who was doing it to get out of studying or if he were struggling at school, I would take a different stance.

Perhaps, if the job didn't pay very much and he was desperate for money, I may pay him in reward for putting in the effort on his studies. Not as a bribe but as a way to earn money for extra study.

A: Agony Aunt. Work can be excellent for confidence, money management techniques, and people skills but it must balance with schoolwork. If you're worried, speak to his teachers to see if they think he can risk taking any time away from his studies. Often having a change of scene for a few hours can help more than hinder, though obviously exam time is particularly critical, and parents have to be firm. I think no more than six to eight hours a week generally and no work for six weeks before exams.

Careers advice

Q: Christopher is a good all-rounder but he does not seem to have a clue about what he wants to do when he finishes school. I feel instinctively that he has a talent with people and should think about the service industries but I am not sure how little/much I should influence/interfere in his decision-making.

A: Pam, mother of two. You can only provide the best opportunities and let him decide, and hopefully make the most of the opportunities given. However, for what it's worth, we did persuade Chris to carry on with the maths element of his degree when he wanted to give it up and now he is Head of Maths.

A: Peter, father of two. You can talk to him about your experiences but put him in touch with professional careers advisers as well. Try to organize some informal work experience for him to get some insight into what a job might entail.

What the experts say

A: Psychiatrist. I suppose again I would want him to have more information and to give him access to this but I wouldn't want to give him any advice unless he asked for it. I would want to find out why he was choosing a certain career, and help him to identify his skills and to see if they match his choice with the help of the school and the careers adviser.

Obviously, you do not want to put a square peg in a round hole. It's all part of helping him to develop his own self-awareness of how and where he fits into the world. It is very important as a parent to be especially careful to separate your hopes and ambitions from his own desires and needs, so that he follows his path, not yours.

A: Agony Aunt. You could take your lead from the school or take on a vocational guidance person. A long view/some common sense is one of the benefits of parenthood and must be shared with your kids. On the other hand, you must have an honest view of your son's potential, and not try to put a square peg in a round hole. Strengths are generally highlighted by successes at school subjects and this generally sets the pace. Having said that, I still don't know what I want to do when I grow up! Many people do degrees in one subject and land up doing something completely different. All part of life's rich pattern, so I wouldn't get too stressed over it.

Dropping out?
Q: My son is bright and does okay at school but he says he has had enough of education. He wants to leave after his GCSEs and I feel that it would be a big mistake. What do you think?

A: Pam, mother of two. Why not encourage him to do a gap year and then re-apply to sixth form college for his A levels? You can't push them to learn so get him to do something useful like Operation Raleigh for example.

A: Lisa, mother of two. Get a teacher that he respects to have a word with him. He might not listen to you but some objective advice from an outsider might be just what he needs.

A: Nick, father of two. I took a year to travel the world on a motorbike with my brother and it was the best thing I ever did.

What the experts say
A: Psychiatrist. I would want to talk it through with him to find out why he feels like that. I'd need to help him to think short term and long term, and to clarify what he wants long term. It might be that having a gap year is the most appropriate thing but, on the other hand, it could stymie his career so I would help him think through that process, and come to the right conclusion.

He might be impatient to explore the world and see new places but sometimes you can point out that if he leaves school without qualifications, he reduces his chances of travelling long term because he is less well educated. You have to look at his long-term objectives.

A: Agony Aunt. If your child is better suited to taking an apprenticeship or learning a skill through indentures, then realize that this might be best for him, especially if he is not a natural academic. Many kids do get fed up with the stress of exams and it is quite natural for them to want to throw in the towel. Most are carried along with their peers when they return to school to continue their studies. Your son's teacher should be enlisted for advice and perhaps encouragement. If your son wants to drop out completely and become a couch potato, you have a problem. You have to hope that he sees sense and returns to some form of education later on. In your dark moments, take hope from Richard Branson who only has one O level and Richard Desmond, proprietor of Express Newspapers, who left school at 15! It's also worth bearing in mind that skilled tradespeople such as plumbers now earn as much as many professional people and are much sought after.

With grateful thanks to Dr Dinah Jayson, child and adolescent consultant psychiatrist, and Charmian Evans, former agony aunt, who are also mothers as well as problem-solving experts. Both of them, coincidentally, have two boys and a girl.

Resources

USEFUL ADDRESSES

Education
The National Association for Gifted Children:
www.nagcbritain.co.uk
Tel: 0845 450 0295

Advice on Children's Education (ACE)
www.ace-ed.org.uk
Tel: 0300 0115 142

Bullying
Kidscape
www.kidscape.org.uk
Helpline: 08451 205 204

Anti-bullying campaign
www.bullying.co.uk
Helpline: 0808 800 222

Street violence
Victim Support
www.victimsupport.org.uk
Support line: 0845 30 30 900

The Suzy Lamplugh Trust
www.suzylamplugh.org
Tel: 0207 091 0014

Drugs and alcohol
Adfam National:
(Confidential advice for families and friends of drug users)
www.adfam.org.uk
Tel: 020 7553 7640

Alcohol concern
www.alcoholconcern.org.uk
National Drink Helpline: 0800 917 8282

UK National Drugs 24-hour Helpline: 0800 77 66 00
Free confidential advice and referral to local services.

The Drug Education Forum
www.drugeducationforum.com
Tel: 0207 739 8494

Sexuality
The Sex Education Forum
www.sexeducationforum.org.uk

British Pregnancy Advisory Service
www.bpas.org
Tel: 0207 627 8962

Brook Advisory Centres.
www.brook.org.uk
24-hour Helpline: 0808 802 1234

Family Planning Association and Information Service
www.fpa.org.uk
Helpline: UK 0845 122 8690
RoI 0845 122 8687

London Lesbian and Gay Switchboard
www.llgs.org.uk
24-hour Helpline: 0300 330 0630

FFLAG (Friend and Family of Lesbians and Gays)
www.fflag.org.uk
Helpline: 0845 652 0311

Stonewall
(An organisation that offers support and advice to young gays)
www.stonewall.org.uk
Infoline: 0800 050 20 20

Terrence Higgins Trust (Aids charity)
Helpline: 0808 802 1221

National AIDS Trust
www.natorg.uk

National Aids Helpline
0800 567 123

Rape Crisis Centres
(Counselling or referral for incest survivors or victims of sexual abuse)
www.rapecrisis.org.uk
Helpline: 0808 802 99 99

Divorce and separation
RELATE
www.relate.org.uk
Tel: 0300 100 1234

National Family Mediation
www.nfm.org.uk

National Stepfamily Association (NSA)
www.londonenquira.co.uk
Tel: 020 7209 2460

Bereavement
CRUSE
www.cruse.org.uk
Helpline: 0844 477 9400

For Single Parents
Gingerbread
(Network of self-help groups for single parents)
www.gingerbread.org.uk
Helpline: 0808 802 0925

Lone Parents
www.lone-parents.org.uk

For Troubled Youngsters
Get Connected
(for youngsters who have run away, been thrown out or who are thinking of running away from home/care)
www.getconnected.org.uk
Helpline: 0808 802 1234

Childline
(Provides a free and confidential service for children and young people)
www.childline.org.uk
24 hour helpline: freephone 0800 1111

Wish-Careline
www.thewishcentre.org.uk
Counselling Line: 020 8514 1177

The Samaritans
www.samaritans.org
 24 hour helpline: UK 08457 90 90 90
RoI 1850 60 90 90

Youth Access
(Support services throughout the UK)
www.youthaccess.org.uk

General Parenting
National Children's Bureau (NCB)
www.ncb.org.uk
Tel: 020 7278 6000

Family Welfare Association
www.fwa.org.uk
Tel: 020 7254 6251

Family Action
www.family-action.org.uk

Parentline Plus
www.familylive.org.uk
Helpline: 0808 800 2222.

NSPCC (National Society for the Prevention of Cruelty to Children)
www.nspcc.org.uk
Helpline: 0800 800 5000

Young Minds
www.youngminds.org.uk
Parent Helpline: 0808 802 5544

National Family & Parenting Institute
www.familyandparenting.org

Working With Men
(materials on boys and literacy, and fatherhood)
www.workingwithmen.org
Tel: 020 7237 5353

12317170R00194

Printed in Great Britain
by Amazon.co.uk, Ltd.,
Marston Gate.